D0883678

Common Sense

❖   ❖   ❖

ALSO BY LAWRENCE E. JOSEPH

Gaia: The Growth of an Idea

Common Sense

❖ ❖ ❖

Why It's No Longer Common

❖ ❖ ❖

Lawrence E. Joseph

A William Patrick Book

Addison-Wesley Publishing Company

Reading, Massachusetts   Menlo Park, California   New York
Don Mills, Ontario   Wokingham, England   Amsterdam   Bonn
Sydney   Singapore   Tokyo   Madrid   San Juan
Paris   Seoul   Milan   Mexico City   Taipei

Library of Congress Cataloging-in-Publication Data

Joseph, Lawrence E.
   Common sense : why it's no longer common /
  Lawrence E. Joseph
     p.   cm.
   "A William Patrick Book."
   ISBN 0-201-58116-7
  1. Common sense. I. Title.
  B105.C457J67 1994
  149–dc20   93-5393
                                          CIP
                                          Rev

Jacket design by Jean Seal
Text design by Joyce Weston
Set in 11-point Galliard by Camden Type 'n Graphics

1 2 3 4 5 6 7 8 9 10-MA-97 96 95 94 93
First printing, December 1993

This book is dedicated to my mother,
Yvonne Joseph,
a person with so much common sense that she
probably wonders if, all in all, the compliment
doesn't make her sound a bit dull.

Contents

Acknowledgments

To Knut Utstein Kloster, of Oslo, Norway, common sense says if you stand tall enough you can look the world, the whole world, right in the eye. I am forever in his debt for boosting me up to take a peek.

I am beholden to Stuart Krichevsky, my literary agent at Sterling Lord Literistic, for being a practical guy with faith beyond reason.

William Patrick, my editor, is the kind of fellow who could throw handfuls of darts and score with darn near all of them. Thanks! Ouch! Thanks!

Introduction:
Whatever Happened to
Common Sense?

Common sense is the good sense that everyone should have. It is the quality of judgment necessary to know the simplest truths, to recognize striking absurdities and to be shocked by palpable contradictions. As sayings go, common sense is the ability to tell your shoes from Shinola, your butt from your elbow, chalk from cheese. Despite what it's called, common sense has always been rare; Will Rogers felt that way, and so does Ross Perot. It is both a baseline requirement and a special attribute, a sine qua non that, in fact, many people lack. To say that someone has good common sense is to pay no small compliment; it implies a sharp eye for the significant, a grasp of the obvious—like seeing the emperor's new clothes—that at times makes everyone else seem colorblind. Or it might simply mean that you have the very good sense to agree with me.

It's as old as the Stone Age, when the first Neanderthals figured out tools. Even older, according to biologists who trace common sense back to the basic survival instincts—avoid predators, find food, take shelter from the storm—that guided the earliest organisms up from the primordial ooze. Over the eons common sense has evolved into our collective perception of reality, the infrastructure of shared beliefs, basic assumptions and rules of thumb that enables us to agree on what's what. Forms of it have existed in every society, and among all races, ages and economic groups.

So whatever happened to it? There's a growing suspicion that common sense is losing influence in the working of the world. Not that people today are any more likely than in the past, say, to put the tomatoes at the bottom of the shopping bag or take motes out of their eyes with pointed objects. But that our ability to observe the world seems to have outpaced our ability to make sense of it, leading to confusion all around. Like trying to drink from a firehose blasting on full, it is entirely possible these days to get drenched with the torrent of facts and images pouring in from all directions and still come away thirstier than ever to know what's really going on.

In "Common Sense as a Cultural System," Clifford Geertz observes that "Religion rests its case on revelation, science on method, ideology on moral passion; but common sense rests its on the assertion that it is not a case at all, just life in a nutshell. The world is its authority." But which world? Not that world "out there" of squandering bureaucrats, rampaging ethnic "cleansers," children bereft of everything except lethal weapons, great forests burned into desert. Geertz must mean the world "in here," the personal world where, knock wood, two and two still equals four.

The premise of this book is that it's not the "sense" so much as the "common" that is changing today. That the world "out there" and the world "in here" are merging uncontrollably, stretching our parameters of commonality to distant and alien places. Contemporary life has become so globalized that remote events have significant and immediate influence on our daily life: Saddam Hussein invades Kuwait and the Sanchez family of Trinidad, Colorado can't sell their home. Running a leaky air conditioner in Italy increases the risk of skin cancer in Australia by depleting the stratospheric ozone layer. Eating a hamburger in Tokyo threatens tropical rain forest in Brazil. An expatriate Hungarian entrepreneur in Canada plays a hunch powerfully and down crashes the British pound. Southern California surfers watch the Weather Channel for South Pacific Ocean disturbances to know when the waves will be up in Del Mar. Another former Yugoslavian republic falls and New York cabbies have to dodge the traffic jams caused by protesters around the U.N. the next day.

But like the Brooklyn Bridge, built more than a hundred years ago and in a lot better shape than most things built since, common sense proudly resists change. Especially for Americans, common sense is rooted in history; it was, after all, our revolutionary battle cry, courtesy of Thomas Paine. Not to say that this heritage has necessarily resulted in an admirably sensible society, any more, say, than Buddhist reverence for nature has yielded ecological paradises in Asia. But that know-how, ingenuity, Moxie, and so on are deeply valued in our culture. In fact, how-to books are, perhaps along with the short story, the only true American literary genre, not for their analytical virtuosity but because of their practical expertise. Common-sense approaches to everything from entrepreneurship to home pickling to auto repair proved that *anything* could be done. Intellectuals may sneer, but if a little plain thinking helps build a watertight ship, who cares if the arguments leak?

"The three great essentials to achieve anything worth while are, first, hard work; second, stick-to-itiveness; third, common sense," wrote Thomas A. Edison.

William Buckley once quipped that he'd rather be governed by the first two hundred names in the Boston telephone directory than by the faculty of Harvard Law School. Conservative pundits from Irving Kristol to Rush Limbaugh have thrilled millions by attacking the "pseudo-academic ideas" of the "liberal intellectual elite." Common sense stands opposed to those whom Saul Bellow calls "high-IQ morons," intellectuals high on their own hot air and dedicated to proving that what clearly is, is not so. Diet doctors and nutritionists who prescribe weird regimens that you know will land you in an emergency room. Economics professors who teach their students that the national debt doesn't matter and that what we really need is the courage to run up some more. Child psychologists who slap disability labels on kids who just need a little more faith in themselves. Even those General Electric engineers who designed the microwave oven that a man named Tony Page of Yorba Linda, California bought. When the bulb burned out in his brand-new oven, Page found no way of screwing in a new bulb without getting a repair service to make a house call. The job took two persons, and cost about $150. Edison would have blown a fuse.

Like George Wallace before him, Ross Perot called them pointy heads instead of morons and assailed the powers that be with a host of homespun metaphors. Wasn't it Perot who, when he was on the General Motors board of directors, said that the best job of driving they do is to run their own company into the ground? The populist maverick delights in skewering a bipartisan elite so highly educated that it consistently outthinks itself, so powerful that it wastes without feeling the pinch, so sheltered that it is, or imagines itself to be, beyond repercussion. Like the glorious coalition that turned highly regulated savings-and-loan institutions into free-market players, creating a class of novice megastakes gamblers, and then covered their losses with our money. Sometimes the sheer inanity of it all parks like a dump truck on the bladder, and then along comes NASA's $30-million space-shuttle toilet, still leaking.

"Stupidity has become as common as common sense was before; and this does not mean that it is a symptom of mass society or that 'intelligent' people are exempt from it. The only difference is that stupidity remains blissfully inarticulate among the non-intellectuals and becomes unbearably offensive among 'intelligent' people," observed philosopher Hannah Arendt in *Understanding and Politics: On the Nature of Totalitarianism* (1951). Writing after Fascism had fallen, and at the start of the Cold War, Arendt argued that common sense is profoundly anti-ideological—it proceeds from practical reality, not prescriptive belief. Today, as we pass from an era of capitalism versus communism versus fundamentalist Islam, we may be entering an era of more sustainable alliances and flexible accommodations. But let's not pop the corks yet. In his April 1991 cover story for *Spy* magazine, James Collins proclaims that "the victory of common sense in nearly all areas of life . . . has been rapid and nearly total. This is the Age of Common Sense." *Spy* is a humor magazine but Collins was not kidding. Common sense told him that?

Here we need a few distinctions in terminology. It is *common knowledge*, for example, that Los Angeles is a smoggy city. *Reference knowledge*, this time from the *Reader's Digest Almanac*, informs us that Los Angeles is the least windy major city in the United States, about 50 percent calmer than average. *Common sense* says that this must be why the smog hardly ever blows away. Taking full advantage of precious fresh-air days, particularly those beautiful City of Angels mornings which follow a night of rain, is *common-sense* (CS) *behavior on a personal level*. CS *behavior at a societal level* would include reducing air pollution by restricting single-passenger automobile travel, open-mall air-conditioning, and other frivolous energy consumption that needlessly pollutes the air. Why then are so many blow dryers operating in a city that hardly ever gets a decent breeze?

Even common sense has its limits. No denying that when it comes to the greatest mysteries, the deepest truths, the most fabulous beauties, as well as the most peculiar customs, a lot more than common sense is required. A common-sense view of the world assumes an objective physical reality that we all share and that exists whether we perceive it or not. It's not all a dream; it's not controlled by wonderful or terrible mythical creatures. If a tree falls in the forest and no one is there to hear it, common sense doesn't care much one way or the other about whether there was a sound.

The secret to common sense is that there is no secret, no guiding philosophy or revelation by which sound, practical thinking can be ensured. It offers little in the way of thrills, transcendent moments or ecstatic sensations.

George Bernard Shaw saw common sense as a cowardly accommodation to the low-energy, zero-inspiration status quo: "A man of great common sense and good taste—meaning thereby a man without originality or moral courage," he writes in his notes to *Julius Caesar*. To the GBS way of thinking, the answer to where common sense has gone is, not far enough.

Although fine scholarly research has been done from Aristotle on down, you can't throw experts at this subject and expect to come up with all the answers. That's the great egalitarian thing about common sense—it's not the property of any party, class, gender, generation, or culture. Of course there are those fundamental principles which transcend all mindsets, but as our world becomes increasingly interdependent, a great many "universal" assumptions are turning out to be nothing more than parochial biases. What's obvious to us may turn out to be just pointless to others, yet with each painful discovery of what really isn't common sense, there comes a new understanding of what we all truly share. Not being a fount of the virtue in question, I found it necessary to go out and examine common sense as it works in the world today.

1

What Are the Limits of Common Sense?

Common Sense Is Not Totally Groovy

"Common sense is thinking necessary, thinking simple, thinking small. And wisdom, pure wisdom, is never having to think at all," explains Heartman, a Lakota Sioux shaman, as he shovels the last of fifty red rocks fresh from the sacred bonfire into the pit just beneath our feet. Fifteen Sioux, Zuñi and Wasichu (whites) were squeezed, women on the right, men on the left, into the sweat lodge, a five-foot swelter dome stitched airtight with hides, furs and ancient prayers. Sacred offerings of tobacco smoke sizzled up from the coals and stung each breath, each glance. We had returned to the crucible of Mother Earth's womb to be purified of our fears, lies, base desires. And in my case, of the terrible tendency to think.

Like awkward ballroom dancers who count 1–2–3, 1–2–3, and look down at their feet, most educated whites lean on logic as a crutch, stilting their minds and hobbling their souls. This is the working assumption of Heartman, a barrel-chested forty-ish father of a dozen from at least three wives or lovers, with a deep charmer's voice and long Sioux braids. The shaman had therefore kindly invited me—for the modest price of $50 that included a night's lodging, three solid meals, and no male-bonding, group drum-beating or "searching for the warrior within"—to the sweat-lodge ceremony to help me "stop living inside my head." Having more than once been accused of analyzing things to death, I accepted his invitation to be healed.

The shaman shut the flap to the tent and plunged us into fetal darkness. Sizzling leg hairs (mine) perfumed the silence. First grumbling, then chanting a mesmerizing monotone, Heartman ladled spring water into the fiery pit. The Steam Spirit hissed and spat like a cat, drenching us, as Dante reported from the most scorching circle of Hell, in sweat hotter than boiling glass. Breathe deeply? Lungs boiled. Shallow? No O_2. The only way to fend off gasping claustrophobia, the only way not to implode psychologically into the pagan pitch, was to forget about yourself and sing along with Heartman instead:

> Hey-ya, Hey-ya. Hey-ya, Hey-ya.
>   La-ka-ta-shi-my-a-na.
> Nnn nnn ohhh ahhh.
>   Common Sense Hey! Common Sense Hey!
> Ham-ble-chay. Ham-ble-chay.
>   Mi-ta-ki-ah-say.

Or something remotely like that. Doesn't matter. For almost two hours the sacred songs saved us all. The Steam Spirit be thanked and praised for not melting us down into one big psychic puddle. God, it felt good to get out of there! I have no idea why I must do it all over again. Heartman thinks I'm making progress.

If unnecessary thoughts are to the mind as wasted movement is to the body, we were all poetry in motion after crawling out of that tent. Go with the flow. Live in the moment. What could be simpler? Common sense was cool night air. Heartman explained that "thinking small, if at all," was like a good driver going down a mountain road, hitting the brakes just occasionally, relying mostly on gearshifting, concentration, and a tight steering wheel. Wisdom, it follows, is never having to hit the brakes at all . . . Although I did notice how carefully Heartman handled the brand-new, fully loaded Jeep Wagoneer that one devotee had given him.

For pending legal reasons, tribal and governmental, the details of Heartman's fundraising methods are best scanted here. Suffice it to say that this less-than-high-school-educated son of an alcoholically dysfunctional reservation family was shrewd and shameless enough to use moving, sacred ceremonies to extract donations and tributes from highly accomplished investment bankers, corporate lawyers and wannabes come to be cured of their cerebral addiction. What common sense really tells Heartman is that people who drive hard for a living will pay through the nose to let someone else do the thinking for them every once in a while.

There is danger in equating common sense with what Robert Pirsig might call the philosophy of the groove. In *Zen and the Art of Motorcycle Maintenance,* Pirsig pillories his character John, the technologically inept traveling companion: "He will not or cannot believe that there is anything in this world for which grooving is not the way to go . . . That's the dimension he's in. The groovy dimension." Pirsig gives an example: When the handlebars of John's gorgeous new BMW motorcycle come loose, he cannot accept the protagonist's fixing them with a strip cut from an aluminum beer can found by the side of the road. That just doesn't fit into this groovy fellow's notion of the way things ought to go with the fine piece of German engineering between his legs, therefore it must be wrong.

Sometimes common sense is intuitive, sometimes planned out step by step. And sometimes it's just remembering to stop and think.

Imagine that it's a wickedly hot and sunny day, and that you're not on a motorcycle but taking the noon bus from Miami up to Jacksonville. Judging from the crowd waiting in line, the bus will be packed, but when you board the beat-up old Greyhound it still has lots of empty seats. Which side of the aisle should you choose?

Assuming that you want to look out the window but also avoid the heat and glare, you would choose the right side of the bus which, as it travels north through Florida, will face east. Facing west, where the sun sets, would expose you to an afternoon of strong sunshine. Easy. For most of us, the problem would not be answering such a question but remembering to ask it in the first place, before instinctively grabbing the shadiest window seat even if that happened to be on the left side while the bus was parked. If you were subconsciously attuned to your geographic orientation—the winds, the movements of the sun, the four directions—as so many Native Americans seem to be, then choosing the correct seat might happen with little or no thought. For most of us though, the common-sense response would be to stop and think not just about where we are at that moment, but where we are going.

Common Sense Can Be a Real Downer

"Common sense is knowing when you've got it good and knowing when you don't," says Tommy Britt, a friend of mine who on his motorcycle flawlessly gauges and compensates for glare, windspeed, surface slicks, and any number of other crucial road variables seemingly without conscious thought.

Tommy is a hedonist, which means he equates pleasure with goodness, and neither of those with work. Time is the capital that life gives you, and your job every day is to invest it wisely enough to reap the profit of pleasure. Failure means failing to be happy. Books, in general, make him unhappy: "To read a whole book on common sense is (no offense) like reading a book on how to walk around," he was forced to conclude of this undertaking. "Maybe a pamphlet or something, okay, but if someone's dipstick is down a whole book, their valves are shot."

To Tommy's way of thinking, reading is kind of like using a slide rule, which was perfectly fine until they invented calculators, or for print, television. For thousands of years people were forced to look at all these squiggles on paper or carved into rocks or whatever, and had to create their own little television programs in their heads. But now that we know how to make real television, why go through all the hassle?

Grooving is the way to go—at the beach, on the bike, with a babe. But Tommy sees no harm in using a beer can to repair his beat-up old Kawasaki 400. If the can comes in handy, that means it's in the groove. Heartman's "think small, if at all" philosophy jibes with his own experience that when things are going well, don't jinx them by analyzing why. But as for sweating your brains out just to stop thinking . . . Tommy has at least a dozen better methods.

Sometimes common sense is just going with what satisfies, even it means crossing your i's and dotting a few t's. In "Deviance as Fun," Wichita State University social psychologist Jeffrey W. Riemer points out that deviant behavior is frequently a "just for the hell of it" activity in which "the participants are engaged simply for pleasure." Riemer, whom I invite for a beer, complains that social psychologists have been too quick to judge people like Tommy as being problem cases, and not just the free spirits they might turn out to be. He argues that "sociologists have neglected to incorporate this hedonistic 'pleasure of the moment' dimension, even though it squares well with a common-sense interpretation for some of the behavior usually recognized as deviant." (It should be noted that Riemer's article appeared in *Adolescence* magazine.)

For Tommy, neglecting pleasure is what leads to sin. He is the only person I have ever known to translate hedonism into foreign policy. Tommy is 100 percent against female circumcision, an ancient, benighted practice prevalent in parts of Africa and the Middle East. Not only is this mutilation barbaric, he argues, but utterly stupid. "Forget decency. If there are still men on this planet who still do not understand that taking away a woman's ability to have sexual pleasure—or worse, causing her pain—radically diminishes his own pleasure, then that culture, forget it. Talk about human rights! We should immediately break off diplomatic relations with any government that allows this to go on."

Never did Tommy have much of a chance to present his policy views, say, to Hillary Rodham Clinton, and that likelihood fell even further recently when he lost his right to vote. Tommy Britt, recovering marijuana dealer, underwent some dramatic philosophical alterations during an eleven-month stretch in the San Diego County jail, where among other things he learned that winning an argument was frequently worse than losing one, and better just to keep his mouth shut.

Prison is far worse for bikers than it is for most of us, like being sentenced to the restroom in a bus. Every moment

Tommy was behind bars, Reason took revenge on the manbeast in which it had the misfortune to be housed, thumping his brain like a kettle drum: DUMB! DUMB! DUMB! DUMB! Common sense, he now says, is also knowing when you've got it really bad.

Common Sense Doesn't Always Play by the Rules

Is it just common sense to legalize marijuana, and perhaps some of the other so-called recreational drugs? No, it's a viable policy option, though far from self-evident. Society has an important stake in limiting the number of citizens sitting around watching television and going "Wow!" at the commercials. But what's criminal is that in some states one might spend more time in jail for possessing an ounce and a half of marijuana than for committing rape or second-degree murder. Tommy got what he deserved: the scare of a lifetime, not the destruction of it.

Common sense behind bars says do whatever you have to to get out in one piece. Consider this CS object lesson learned by another errant friend of mine; call him Louie. As a first offender, Louie had been sentenced to two and a half years in the Ohio state penitentiary for armed robbery, knocking over a candy store. The day before Louie started serving his sentence, his father went up to the prison with $5,000 in cash he had gotten from an emergency home-equity loan. He then proceeded to spread it around to guards, inmates—the right people, whom he had learned about by asking around at his union hall—with one instruction: that his son should come out with the same sexual history he went in with. Another $5,000 would be payable upon his son's healthful emergence. Louie made parole on his first try, came out anally intact, and his father paid up. After taking 10 G's worth out of that stupid kid's hide, Louie's father got him into a construction trade union, and now

Louie is sitting pretty as a crane operator, earning an impressive hourly wage.

Some fathers would have taken to drink, others to depression and denial, others to psychotherapy. A frightening number wouldn't have given a damn either way. The diligent paterfamilias might have visited often and worked closely with prison social workers. But Louie's father had sense enough to know that "money talks, bullshit walks" and he did the smart, practical thing.

Laws are like the lines painted on the road, to the CS way of thinking. Ninety-nine percent of the time you stay within them, but you have the absolute right to ignore them to avoid an accident. Most legal systems recognize that exceptions are sometimes necessary, but few go so far as the U.S. Coast Guard, which explicitly sets common sense above its own regulations. In *Navigation Rules,* the "General Prudential Rule" states that "attention shall be given to all hazards of navigation, threats of collision, or special circumstances that may require a departure from the customary procedures to avoid immediate danger. . . . In other words, *common sense* [italics mine] must always accompany the application of the Navigation Rules, and you must do everything you can to avoid a collision, even if it involves breaking the rules." The general prudential rule has stood up in court, where boat owners who adhered to the letter of the law but failed to use common sense have been found at fault. The Coast Guard manual sensibly adds, "The best time to know the Rules (and the worst time to study them) is when a collision is imminent."

That advice holds for all sorts of emergencies, like when you hit a patch of ice on the road and start skidding to the right. Except in that situation, common sense, which says yank the wheel to the left, can get you killed. Driver's education teaches us to resist the natural response, and to turn right, into the skid, and thereby avoid spinning or flipping the car. Similarly, when caught out in the freezing cold for a very long time, what could be more sensible than warming up fast as you can as soon as you get inside? Yet slower, gentler warming is a lot safer, because a rapid rise in body temperature may demand that too much blood be delivered to remote areas of the body too quickly, rupturing the heart.

Common sense sometimes seems that way only in retrospect. We all know the feeling of belated epiphany, accompanied by a palm-slap to the forehead and the honest admission that really, we should have known it all along. Or maybe with the slightly less frank contention that the answer, in fact, was always on the tip of our tongue. There was a great scene in *Raiders of the Lost Ark,* where the main character, Indiana Jones, is trying to escape from endless murderous thugs in some utterly exotic bazaar, and out jumps this strapping big foe, whipping crescent swords around like a champion baton twirler, challenging Jones to a duel. The rules of the action adventure-genre say the hero should take up his sword and slay the evil expert at his own deadly game. The audience expected it; the villain expected it. But Jones simply pulled out his revolver and blew him away. No big deal. That's just common sense, which Harvard psychologist Ellen Langer calls "mindfulness," an intellectual virtue that she energetically vaunts in a book of the same name. The Indiana Jones character was alert enough to avoid what Langer would consider "acting from a single perspective"—mindlessly accepting the terms set down.

It takes more than common sense to make up your own rules and then get everyone else to play along. Since the dawn of recorded history, the cornerstone assumption of philosophy, psychology and education has been, basically, the more consciousness the better. Knowledge is power and the truth shall set you free. Ronald Reagan knew better.

Reagan was a master of the art of strategic ignorance; he was mindful that one must not appear to be overly mindful. The most popular American president since FDR had the good sense not to know anything more than he had to, if that much, and the good taste not to show it if he did. The American public could never really be sure that their commander-in-chief wasn't, in fact, totally unaware of a major, even globally critical, situation. Remember when his advisors didn't wake him up for the dogfight over Libya? One of the most beloved leaders of the twentieth century, he still cheerfully admits to a chancy memory and to disdain for the details of governance. To Reagan, facts are like pennies in this wealthy information age: only the poor have to keep track of them.

Reagan had enough sense to realize that the less aware one seems, the more freedom one has to lie. Sure, the Gipper exchanged a few salutes over the years with Oliver North, and probably did tell the handsome young lieutenant colonel to carry on with whatever. But would Reagan keep track of a hypercomplicated plan that somehow involved Nicaragua, Iran, Israel, Swiss banks, money laundered through the Sultan of Brunei, and the CIA running drugs? Plus, if George Schultz and Bill Moyers were to be believed, George Bush and the savings-and-loan scandal? Unlike his failure of a predecessor, Jimmy Carter, Ronald Reagan was not the kind of commander-in-chief to get bogged down in minutiae. It is entirely plausible that of the 150 questions submitted in his Iran-Contra testimony, Reagan's 124 "I don't recall's" were stated honestly, and with some pride.

Nixon must still be shaking his head. If his administration had gotten caught running a diabolically convoluted scheme like

Iran-Contra, the whole world would have assumed that Tricky Dick was at the helm. Remember the Watergate-era bumper sticker, "Honk if You Think He's Guilty"? As the truth of the matter became painfully obvious, driving with one of those stickers was like being chased by a gaggle of angry geese. Mitchell, Haldeman, Erlichman et al. might conceivably have hidden the initial break-in from their leader, but Nixon was such a shrewd, crafty man that no one could believe he didn't know—and deny—the essential details of coverup. Nixon was too sharp not to know. Had Reagan been president he would have claimed that the whole Watergate thing happened during his nap, chastised a few of his loyal patriots for their misguided zeal, and then really nodded off after a job well done.

Common Sense Is No Match for Hormones

Buddy Cianci, who when mayor of Providence, Rhode Island, was widely believed to have accosted his wife's lover, beat him with a fireplace log, tortured him with lit cigarette butts, then called up his pal the former Attorney General to brag about it all, may not be the model of common sense. But then again, Cianci, who was convicted of felonious assault and removed from office, did get reelected. The people of Providence, capital of the state *The New York Times* once dubbed "the land that time forgot," understood the timeless truth that in matters of heart and groin, anyone can lose his head. As for Cianci, he learned this much of a common-sense lesson: "I would have been more discreet next time."

That phrase, worthy of Yogi Berra, is something Dr. Gary Lewis, of Harrisburg, Pennsylvania, should have tatooed on his forehead. Here are the sordid facts: Lewis, a successful, married osteopathic obstetrician/gynecologist, met Molly Bartlett in a York County massage parlor in 1985 and for three and a half years carried on a relationship with her, at the price of $100 an hour. In 1989, Bartlett agreed to become Lewis's exclusive mistress and the two parties jointly purchased a house, he putting in $70,000, she, $10,000, where she alone would live. (He continued to reside with his wife in their mansion in a fashionable part of town.) Two months later, the property was transferred solely into Bartlett's name—he claims it was to avoid gift taxes, she, more convincingly, in exchange for her promise not to sue him for having given her a venereal disease. After a violent spat, she barred him from the house altogether.

All this would have remained quiet and unprintable had not Dr. Lewis, a man of standing in the state capital, with a marriage and professional practice to consider, decided to sue to get his $70,000 back. He pressed his claim all the way through trial, basing much of his case on (pun unavoidable) his right to "residential easement." To the undying gratitude of the local news media, the case decided by Judge John C. Dowling, filed in the Pennsylvania Court of Common Pleas as "The Tale of the Dispossessed Doctor, or Mistress Molly and Her Lover's Folly" 3578-S-1989, made Lewis one of the biggest laughing stocks in the commonwealth's history.

The sagas of Cianci and Lewis may seem destined for the annals of utter stupidity, but to the ancient Romans they would have made perfect common sense. According to an essay by Paul Veyne, in *A History of Private Life: From Pagan Rome to Byzantium* (Belknap/Harvard, 1987): "In Rome . . . common sense held that the world was perverted and decadent. It was also believed that morality consists not in the love or habit of virtue but in having the strength to resist vice. . . . Everyone took these facts for granted, and philosophers claimed to derive them from their doctrines or, in perfect good faith, bolstered their doctrines with the teachings of common sense." In other words, we all have the same fundamental propensity to go nuts like Cianci and Lewis; it's just that most of us have, through education and experience, developed the strength to resist.

The Roman notion that human beings are inherently perverse eventually evolved into the Christian doctrine of original sin, formulated by Augustine of Hippo, the party hearty saint who, when the Lord called him to service, answered, "Give me chastity and continence, but not just now," and then partied on for another year. St. Augustine confessed that "I was in love with loving," realized that it was a universal problem, and blamed it all on Adam's corrupted semen. "In Adam's fall, we sinn'd all," has always been an excellent excuse. Today we may put less stock in Adam's seminal influence than in Leakey's Lucy, the evolutionary mother of us all, whose mitochondrial DNA each of us is said to be carrying. Yet which theory, sin or DNA, explains more about the frailty of the human character, the Cianci-Lewis phenomenon? Or about the peculiar urgency that impelled the commissioners of St. John's County, Florida, to compose this statutory definition:

"Buttocks. The area at the rear of the human body which lies between two imaginary lines running parallel to the ground when a person is standing, the first or top of such line drawn at the top of the cleavage of the nates (i.e. the prominence formed by the muscles running from the back of the hip to the back of the leg) and the second or bottom line of this cleavage or the lowest point of the curvature of the fleshy protuberance, whichever is lower, and between two imaginary lines on each side of the body, which lines are perpendicular to the ground and to the horizontal lines described above, and which perpendicular lines are drawn through the point at which each nate meets the outer side of each leg." This bit of anatomical gerrymandering is part of an ordinance designed to keep nude dancing out of St. Augustine, the city named in honor of the venerable theologian. Our tax dollars at work. Amen.

COYOTE, an advocacy group for legalized prostitution, used to have a very CS motto: "My Ass Is My Own!" Not that nude dancing and prostitution are at all the same profession, but the slogan's common-sense principle seems to apply—if you've got a nice butt, and somebody wants to see it, then you should have the right to wave it around.

Seeking the opinion of someone with a more personal stake in this issue, I consulted Angie (her stage name), an old friend of a friend who over the years has worked periodically as an exotic dancer. She got a kick out of the "fleshy protuberance" part, wanted a copy of the ordinance for her act, but then grew suspicious upon learning that my real motive was common sense:

"Just as long as common sense doesn't mean I have to wear sensible shoes," she replied, cautiously.

What worries Angie is the relentless assault on her body and personal freedom in the name of common sense. Bigger breasts mean bigger bucks, the dance-club owners argue, meanwhile pressuring small-breasted dancers to get cosmetic implants. What with all those fashion models sprouting from one lingerie catalogue to the next, the whole idea of implants has gotten the equivalent of a *Good Housekeeping* seal of approval. Some clubs have become very aggressive, requiring and occasionally even financing implant surgery. They tell the dancers it's like getting a capital improvement, since the girls can go anywhere they want after the operation is paid off. And the breasts, of course, they get to keep.

"But look closely at those full-breasted girls . . ." wrote Jane Mulvaugh in her spirited inaugural column as fashion editor of *The European* newsweekly, ". . . aside from their pneumatic bosoms, aren't they still narrow-hipped and lean-legged? Their voluptuousness is an illusion ... a surgical contrivance, an anatomical lie." Angie shrugs off the moral indignation and comments that implants open career opportunities for girls who would otherwise have to work some straight job for a living, meaning more competition for her.

"It's weird because they don't move the same way with the dancer's body. But what gets me about implants is that you go to all this trouble of surgery and everything to make yourself more attractive, and then you can't enjoy it when it works." She's referring to the fact that implants can reduce sensitivity and generally make the recipient more cautious and self-conscious about how her breasts are handled. A very CS argument, though I didn't insult her by saying so.

Common Sense Is No Substitute for Style

Common sense is small potatoes, a bran muffin for breakfast, double coupons on Wednesday, long underwear in winter even if it makes you look bulky, no-label blue jeans, his-and-hers bicycle helmets, short hair in summer, SPF 15, a Timex watch, Lite beer, what Sears used to make, an ox instead of a horse, buying another Honda Accord, the little engine that could, pulling up weeds, getting out the phone book instead of calling directory assistance, sacrificing a runner to second base rather than swinging away, passing off the basketball when you're double-teamed, getting up fifteen minutes earlier so that you don't have to rush around in the morning.

All in all it's short on style, a little heavy on the starch.

Much of what we call common sense comes in managing the dreary necessity from which the social elite are privileged to be spared. On a rainy day it is a good idea to carry an umbrella but it's an even better idea to have your personal assistant take care of those things. To the likes of Leona Helmsley, the empress with new clothes, common sense is for the little people, the Joe Sixpacks, after their ruminative belch. Yet to people who truly have little, who'd love a sixpack but who'll settle for the returnable empties, common sense often means a way of thinking that is supposed to make sense to them but doesn't: Thanks for the umbrella, but we were really thinking more in terms of something with a roof.

"Common sense, in so far as it exists, is all for the bourgeoisie. Nonsense is the privilege of the aristocracy. The worries of the world are for the common people," wrote drama critic George Jean Nathan, in his *Autobiography of an Attitude*. (Nathan's sidekick was H. L. Mencken, whose famous "No one ever went broke underestimating the taste of the American public" some people take to be ironic.) Common sense tends, as Aristotle believed all good tends, toward the middle, and the middle tends toward the suburbs, where neither Leona nor the little people feel very much at home.

Suburban life is a masterpiece of compromise, and compromise is a very commonsensical thing to do. The quintessential American lifestyle offers the best blend of country and city, refuge and convenience thus far achieved by any known civilization. Plastic patio furniture that can be adjusted to one's comfort and left out in the rain without the worry of mildew. Quick-melting Kraft *Old English* American cheese, each slice individually wrapped for safety and freshness, unlike those bulky gourmet cheeses, which, of course, are also widely available. Snubnosed minivans, among the first to be equipped with remote-control door unlockers that yelp like a stepped-on pup, are ideal for kid hauling, carpooling and teenage love. What a thrill of empowerment it must be the first time a lucky tot gets to press the button for the garage-door opener, or deactivate the burglar alarm!

Until recently, however, there was a flaw in suburban commonsensicality, right in the car. When the summer sun beats down on a parked automobile, the seats get hot, the steering wheel gets hot, the interior gets insufferably stuffy. If you're wearing shorts or a short dress, the backs of your thighs burn and stick to the upholstery. The air conditioner offers no immediate relief and in fact usually starts by blowing out hot air. Some ultra-luxury cars now offer systems that can be programmed to cool your car on battery power ten minutes before you return, but these are extremely expensive and wasteful. What else can you do?

Why not stick something in the windshield to block out the sunshine? This is what Avi Fattal and his partner, Avi Ruimi, figured when they started up Auto-Shade, Inc. in Los Angeles. Actually, the simple, accordion-folded cardboard devices, held in place by sunvisors, had been sold in their native Israel for years, so the businessmen improved and adapted them for the American market. For less than $5 at retail, these simple, durable, lightweight sunscreens really keep a car from heating up inside, a sensible solution to a common problem. So why did it bomb when first introduced in the States?

"Until we hit on the right design the Auto-Shade was just a piece of cardboard. It was like trying to sell boxes," said Fattal. Common sense took them just so far. It was only after they stenciled a pair of Michael Jackson-type sunglasses on the front of each shade, and positioned their product as "Sunglasses for Your Car" that sales took off. Common sense, southern California style. "Every time the news interviewed us, they would ask how many Auto-Shades we sold. If our target was five million, we would say we sold five million. Then for the next interview, of course, we would have to say we sold even more," laughs Fattal, confessing that he really has no idea how many they sold. But now both Avis are millionaires. Common sense, Israeli style.

"Common sense is answering a problem the way that someone without emotional attachment would answer it. Most of the time you would get the right answer," says Fattal. But the fact is that being objective generally means agreeing with him. An extremely relaxed and amiable individual, Fattal nonetheless says everything with a tone that Clifford Geertz calls "an air of of-courseness," a this-is-the-way-it-is quality that Geertz considers the fundamental stylistic feature of common sense. Fattal's commanding manner derives in part from his military experience. (To preclude possible reprisals, former Israeli soldiers are sensibly advised not to discuss their duty publicly.) Suffice it that if Fattal taught a management course it would be Seize 101. He sees American higher education as something of a common-sense extraction system, and when his wife Janet—teacher, screenwriter and doting mother—makes a mistake, he teases her, saying, "That's your Master's degree." (She agrees that common sense is "something that educated people never seem to have enough of," but her heart is in literature, art and other realms far beyond the pragmatic.)

Fattal's digs get a lot sharper when it comes to the legion of M.B.A.s who seem to learn everything about money except how to make enough of it. "To me this is very stupid because money is not very interesting to think about or talk about. It is interesting to have." His one investment tip: "Buy Israeli real estate. It's a small country getting smaller."

After selling out to Ruimi and a brief wife-crazing "retirement" at age thirty, Fattal hit it big once again with his "common sense and then some" approach. "One night some friends and I wanted to go out and play pool, but everywhere we went was crowded. And these pool halls, you know, you really had to like this game to enjoy being there. They were not such nice places. So . . ." He follows with a "the-rest-is-history" shrug.

The rest, specifically, is Q's, a billiards bar and restaurant on Los Angeles's fashionable Wilshire Boulevard. The common-sense part was recognizing that crowded pool halls meant lots of demand; the "then some" was going the shabby pool halls one better by creating an attractive, contemporary atmosphere, with videos, a hot deejay, and unlike its smoky forebears, plenty of light and air. That neither he nor any of his partners had ever been in the restaurant business before did not faze Fattal: "We wanted a simple, limited menu, everything high quality," an accomplishment reflected in favorable local reviews. The pan pizza is particularly well known because it is served free to the customers who, ever since Q's opened in 1986, have waited in lines averaging half an hour on many weeknights, twice that or more on weekends. This pool hall became chic! Recently a second Q's opened in Pasadena, a wildly popular multi-story entertainment emporium that, together with the original, seems destined to spin off a national franchise. Make that, international franchise.

Common Sense Doesn't Know How Much to Believe

The simplest explanation generally being the best, odds are that there is no God, gods, cosmic justice, reincarnation, hereafter or firmament of heaven. The basic common-sense assumption is that the universe has no mind, goals, intentions, plans or agendas. It just is, and that's that. Yet that which may be common sense to assume is not necessarily common sense to believe. Why tempt fate, or forfeit an option, especially one that might lead to inner bliss or even everlasting life? Odds are that the odds can be beaten, if you know how. From time immemorial, enough worthy individuals, perhaps a majority, have believed in a higher power. Why not worship "just in case"—He, She, or Hesh would have to be less than human not to appreciate a good sacred offering, even if absolute sincerity was not part of the package. Then again, common sense also says there's got to be a better way of spending your time than making meaningless propitiations to nonexistent deities—like doing good works, or just having a good time, here on Earth.

Archie Bunker put it best when he put his foot in it: "Religion is what nobody in their right mind would believe in," a declaration that somehow was intended to confirm his absolute faith. Neither Archie nor common sense are up to the big questions of the eternal, almighty or sublime. This much is self-evident, that a CS understanding of the world cannot come from belief in the infallibility of any one book or creed. How could it? The only truth that unites all sacred texts, from the Bible to the Koran to the Tibetan Book of the Dead, is that there is not a single intentional laugh among them. Ironically, the grim fanatics of all faiths have together created a common-sense theology by default, which is skeptical irreverence for anyone who presumes to speak for the Almighty.

"Set your minds on things that are above, not on things that are on earth, for you have died, and your life is hidden with Christ in God," wrote Paul in his letter to the Colossians (3:1–4). Belief in God, my custom, can overwhelm conventional notions of cause and effect. At times it is as Paul describes, a glorious, transcendent experience. But not when others have set their minds so firmly on things above that they run right over lowly you. Once during the 1980 Democratic National Convention in New York, I had to walk down from the fourteenth floor because the hotel's elevators, jammed to capacity by the convention crowd, simply would not come. The emergency stairwell was desperately hot and sweaty. Just ahead of me was an elderly woman, up from Mississippi with a Christian group, carrying a large, heavy suitcase. I offered and she accepted that I carry it down. All the way down she praised the Lord for her good fortune. In the lobby, I gave her the suitcase, and she praised the Lord again. By her standards, she had not been negligent or rude—I was what God had delivered and merited no more thanks than a handtruck.

Moses, Jesus, Buddha, Muhammad, and of course God Himself—most of the world's great prophets and deities are men. Mary is sacred as the holy mother of Jesus, though more as an intermediary than unto herself. Today feminist spirituality seeks to elevate a woman to that pantheon: Gaia, the Greek goddess of Earth; Shekinah from the Judaic Kabbalah; Wicca, of pagan witchcraft. In her bestseller, *The Goddess in Everywoman,* Jean Shinoda Bolen argues effectively that the concept of the goddess within is a rhetorical tool that, at its simplest, helps women engender and focus self-esteem. Conceivably it may also enable devotees to commune with the divine. Whatever the ultimate realities, the Earth-bound spirituality of goddess worship seems at least as reasonable as traditional skyward reverence.

On the whole, though, common sense does seem a bit left-brained from the New-Age perspective, that blend of theories on metaphysics and human potential which stresses the unity of nature and manifests itself in such apparently disparate areas as holistic medicine, ecological politics, goddess art and freelance spirituality. Those who would rolf, psycho-channel, out-of-body catapult or otherwise Shirley-MacLaine their way to enlightenment are beyond the CS orbit. Not that these luminati don't emanate bounteous karma. Just that as far as common sense goes, theirs went cosmic.

Belief is not inherently commonsensical, and neither is denial, particularly when it is dogma. Through its organ, *The Skeptical*

Inquirer, CSICOP (Committee for the Scientific Investigation of Claims of the Paranormal) doggedly showers cold water on notions of psychic phenomena, UFOs, telepathy and anything else it deems "pseudoscience." To these high-profile hardheads— including Carl Sagan, B. F. Skinner, Isaac Asimov, Nobel laureate physicist Murray Gell-Mann, DNA discoverer F. H. C. Crick (but not Watson), and the crusading magician James Randi— common sense is whatever induces the suggestible lay public to reject unauthorized claims.

Sci-cops believe in Science with a capital S. They wink at the perverse anomalies of quantum physics such as the Einstein-Podolsky-Rosen paradox (see Chapter 5), where sister particles created from the same chance collision are considered to be so intimately linked together—even at opposite sides of the universe—that if one spins one way, the other's got to spin the other way. But any connection between a mother waking up frightened in her bed at about the same moment that, somewhere out on the highway, her child has been in a car crash is, of course, just a coincidence.

Common sense isn't much help in sorting out what's just a coincidence and what's really a whole lot more. In *Innumeracy: Mathematical Illiteracy and Its Consequences* (1988), CSICOP fellow John Allen Paulos aptly points out that this is "an increasingly complex world full of senseless coincidences." Paulos argues that with the information explosion, the incidence of meaningless correspondences and chance identicalities is bound to increase accordingly. There are that many more chances for coincidences to happen. "The paradoxical conclusion is that it would be very unlikely for unlikely events not to occur." Yet in *The Roots of Coincidence* (Random House, 1973) Arthur Koestler refutes the probabilistic standard of proof, predictability: a mother should know it every time a child has a car crash, or at least much more frequently than sheer guesswork would yield. "But it is in the very nature of parapsychological phenomena that they are *not* repeatable at will, and that they operate unpredictably. This is the issue which has bedeviled the controversy from its very beginnings." Even if it happened only once, that mother could still have sensed something real.

CSICOP is like the guy who, very intelligently but with a gratuitously vicious edge, points out what a fool you are for believing you can beat the odds. In "Science and Commonsense Skepticism" (Fall 1991), John Aach, a software consultant turned health-care expert for the occasion, tries to debunk the field of hypnotism, a CSICOP no-no, and in doing so quacks like a duck. Aach describes a woman smoker who, while attending a hypnotist's clinic on quitting, peeked when her eyes were supposed to be closed, and saw the hypnotist standing in front of her, sucking air through his teeth. After a second session several days later and with instructions to visualize coffee or some other pleasurable substitute whenever the urge to smoke hit, Madame X reported that her urge to smoke had significantly decreased, for which she gave the hypnotist "considerable credit."

Her gratitude annoys Aach no end: "*Everyone* [italics his] knows the limits of the effects in the everyday world of cups of coffee and sucking air through one's teeth . . ." sniffs Aach. The usual knock on hypnotherapy is that the suggestions wear off after a while, and patients relapse. But Aach makes no such contention, arguing only that the hypnotist deserves no credit for helping Madame X beat her addiction because she felt no reduction in her desire to smoke until almost a week after the first treatment, "when the worst withdrawal symptoms might have passed on their own."

This is sledgehammer science masquerading as common sense. As someone who smoked a pack a day for ten years, I am painfully aware that though physical addiction to nicotine may disappear after several days of abstinence, the agony of desire does *not* (italics mine and many millions of other smokers' and ex-smokers') necessarily diminish after "almost a week," and in fact can return with a vengeance after the initial resolve to quit fades. (Perhaps Aach, who works for the John Hancock Mutual Insurance Company, where they undoubtedly know a great deal about the consequences of smoking, might be expected to be up on this subject.)

If a hypnotist helps people kick a disgusting, life-threatening habit by making air-sucking sounds through his teeth, so be it. As it happens, one image that helped me a lot was that of a breeze through my mind, blowing away smoky desires. Hokey, but that little breath of fresh air, not unlike the sensation that might have been created by Madame X's hypnotist, has helped hundreds of times over the seven years since I quit. Perhaps if someone had suggested that image—even better, had somehow figuratively implanted it into my consciousness as hypnotists attempt to do—I might have quit a lot sooner. Aach reports no follow-up on the hypnotist or Madame X, and so we can assume he did not seek her out to (dis)abuse her of the treatment's success.

As we shall see, yesterday's common sense frequently becomes today's pat assumption and tomorrow's obsolete thought. It's the caboose on the intellectual train. But trains, these days, streak silently at 200 mph, tilt so that they can go faster around turns, and use fuzzy logic to brake impeccably to a halt. In this book we will examine how common sense is changing with the approach of the third millennium and how, like a conductor blowing the whistle to warn drivers that the train is crossing the road, some things about common sense always remain the same.

2

How Does Common Sense Work?

We are stuck in a supermarket checkout line when out from behind the wire magazine rack jumps this headline:

LONE STAR LUNACY! ECCENTRIC TEXAS GENIUS SPENDS $35 MILLION TO TEACH HIS COMPUTER HOW TO READ SUPERMARKET TABLOIDS!

All that money to try to convince a computer that the two-headed boy in India just cut one of them off, and is now on trial for its murder? Or that Elvis, 57, now married and living in a suburb of Memphis, just paid a visit to his new grandson?

"It's the best way there is for my machine to learn common sense!" says science whiz Douglas Lenat.

Strange but true: since 1984, Douglas Lenat and his team of artificial intelligence (AI) researchers at the Microelectronics and Computer Technology Corporation (MCC) in Austin, Texas have invested nearly $35 million and 200 person-years of research in an attempt to program their supercomputer "Cyc," as in en-*cyc*-lopedia, with the equivalent of human common sense. This is by far the largest study of common sense, computer-associated or otherwise, in history.

"My hope is that before this century is out that no one could think of buying a computer without Cyc any more than anyone would now think about buying a computer without word processing," says Lenat, who has held faculty positions at Carnegie-Mellon University, and at Stanford, where he remains a consulting professor.

Common sense at Computerland by Christmas 2000, on 3 ½ inch disks? The odds are against it, though not against Cyc doing a much better imitation than almost anyone thought (hoped?) possible for a mindless machine. Regardless of Cyc's ultimate prospects, the project is immediately valuable for the opportunity it presents to take an objective look at common sense, to see what a grasp of the obvious is made of, how the parts of practical reasoning fit. The Cyc project is particularly valuable to the student of common sense because each step Cyc takes toward common-sense awareness happens as though in slow-motion video, freeze-framed thought after painstaking thought. Machines begin their existence as empty metal vessels with no motivation to learn: they must be taught *everything,* and everything they are taught must be made absolutely explicit.

Despite more than two-thousand years of scholarly scrutiny, only since the 1960s, when AI researchers first tried and failed to teach computers to think like people, has the paradox of common sense been driven home: the mental tasks we find simplest usually turn out to be the most complex in the knowledge, reasoning skills, and brainpower used. Who would have guessed that even the most advanced expertise is child's play compared to common sense? It has been almost forty years since software was developed to solve calculus problems far beyond the capability of the human brain but it will probably be another forty, at least, before computers figure out how to play hop-scotch, pass notes and otherwise do what an average child might do during a day at kindergarten.

"Common sense is not a simple thing. Instead, it is an immense society of hard-earned practical ideas—of multitudes of life-learned rules and exceptions, dispositions and tendencies, balances and checks," writes Marvin Minsky in *The Society of Mind* (1986). Minsky, one of Lenat's mentors and supporters, has studied common sense since late in the 1960s at MIT's Artificial Intelligence Laboratory. He explains why something as obvious and natural as common sense is actually so intricate and obscure: "This illusion of simplicity comes from losing touch with what happened during infancy, when we formed our first abilities. As each new group of skills matures, we build more layers on top of them. As time goes on, the layers below become increasingly remote." In other words, we adults have forgotten how complicated learning common sense really was.

Though a fascinating discovery, the perverse complexity of common sense has not been good news for the artificial-intelligence funding powers that be, many of whom blithely assumed that teaching computers the rudiments of reasoning would be about as difficult as sending a dog to obedience school, and not too much more expensive. Minsky, AI's leading apologist, has had lots of practice explaining why this dog just won't heel: "Thousands, and perhaps millions of little processes must be involved in how we anticipate, imagine, plan, predict and prevent—and yet all this proceeds so automatically that we regard it as 'ordinary common sense.'" When a child tries to build a tower of blocks higher, how does she know that she shouldn't take out a block already being used? How does noticing that the blocks all fall down become a rule for the next pile of blocks, or for when it's time to stack up all her coloring books and games? Minsky reports that this stacking problem baffled MIT's robot, called Builder, for many months.

Led by Roger Penrose, a mathematical physicist at Oxford University and author of the bestselling, *The Emperor's New Mind* (1989), and John Searle, a cognitive philosopher at the University of California at Berkeley, a chorus of critics point to nearly half a century of failure. They charge that computers simply cannot be conscious in the way that our minds are, and that they therefore will never make anything but a pale imitation of human intelligence. Common sense is seen as a fundamental competence built upon the cumulative discoveries of our ancestors, a genetic and cultural inheritance hundreds of generations in the making.

Artificial intelligence's defenders dismiss these criticisms as human chauvinism. If animals can master such anthropocentric skills as reading and ordering random numerals on a computer screen, as rhesus monkeys have done in a matter of weeks, or can grasp analogies—if a bat is related to a ball, and a ball is related to a glove, then a bat is also related to a glove—as sea lions have been trained to do, why assume that the ability to reason is solely the human domain? Dolphins are so clever that some researchers believe they themselves have, on occasion, been the subjects of experiments devised by the inquisitive whales. Even ants, according to Harvard biologist E. O. Wilson, have the basics: "If common sense means living by a set of rules of thumb which have worked well in the past, but living without examining those rules too closely or in detail, then, yes, ants have common sense. Collectively, but not individually."

The difference, of course, is that animals and insects are alive. But what law says that a mind needs to be made of protein in order to think? AI's proponents argue that consciousness is a matter of the proper programming, whether it's in brain cells, silicon chips, or any other medium that can process the information. But the (crushing) burden of proof is on them.

As a young scientist, Lenat learned the limits of senseless intelligence when he won renown for his computer program called AM, which sifted through a set of standard mathematical concepts and eventually came up with an original theorem about prime numbers and their function as factors. Although AM won him the professionally prestigious Computers and Thought award in 1977, and was the main reason *Science Digest* in 1984 named him one of America's brightest scientists under forty, Lenat quickly grew dissatisfied with his award-winning approach. He concluded that a computer without common sense is like an unwinding spring: "The learning you get out of these programs is really only what you preengineer into them. . . . In 1983 I got this vision about what was holding back the program: it lacked common sense," says Lenat in an interview with *Discover* magazine.

But why teach common sense to computers in the first place? Granted, the pursuit of knowledge is its own justification in this gluttonous Information Age, but what would make anyone spend all that time and money to pick apart common sense into a zillion pieces and then try to put it back together again? It's not like common sense has to be fixed. Why supercomputerize what works perfectly well without any gizmos at all? Wouldn't it be like teaching Builder the robot to dance the ballet? An incredible trick, no doubt, but beyond showing off, what's the point?

Cyc's ostensible purpose is to protect us from the mindless computer goofs and glitches that can with nanosecond suddenness disrupt communications, short-circuit power grids, erase bank accounts, and so on. But a flip through the supermarket tabloids being fed to Cyc's brain makes one wonder if Lenat doesn't have a more elaborate defense system in mind. It says here that alien space doctors are doing secret experiments on patients in hospitals, with the aim of modifying human beings for their own purposes. And that a killer plant has just eaten a very nice lady from Alabama. Page after page of the outrageous, bizarre and just plain idiotic. Even the charge that President Clinton flies in UFOs with his alien masters seems less of a leap than the jump from common sense to Lenat's favorite scandal sheets.

"It's a great source. . . . When you read a headline with an absurd premise, it's easy to then ask yourself, 'What do I know that causes me to doubt this?' " he explains in an interview with *MIS News,* a computer-industry trade journal. Somehow this explanation is reminiscent of the clergyman who, upon being caught with a stash of hard-core pornography, declared, "To preach against evil, one must know it." The argument has a certain reverse logic, but there's also the danger of getting carried away. It seemed like a good idea to invest in a few tabloids, then pay a visit to Lenat and find out what in Sam Hill's going on.

The Common-Knowledge Roundup

Compared to the rest of Texas, Austin is hilly, green, a fair-to-middling walking-around town with a beautiful old historical district that dates from the Lone Star days. Being the state capital and main campus of the University of Texas, Austin does have its eggheads, techies and bureaucrats, but they blend right in.

It's not until the security guard politely insists on accompanying you to the bathroom that you realize Microelectronics and Computer Technology Company is not just another hi-tech chip factory where they mostly bother themselves about who's tracking in dirt. This advanced computer-technology research and development consortium is statutorily limited to U.S. and Canadian companies. (Even though it's located just a few hours north of the border, Mexican companies, alas, are not invited.) Kodak, Digital Equipment Corporation, Apple, Bellcore, US West and NCR provide much of the basic funding, and the rent is paid from the University of Texas's massive endowment. A flower of late-stage postindustrial capitalism is MCC, though by no means is it a free-market competitor.

To Lenat, a roly-poly, fluorescent-pale, early middle-aged supernerd with megawatt vitality, the newcomer is just another text, albeit in human form, to be perused. (I yielded up an early, unedited version of the opening paragraph of this book, which may be gumming up Cyc's cogitators even now.) Once scanned, one's task is to listen, and to indicate periodically that one understands what is being said. Such deportment would be insupportable from most anyone else, but Lenat's sparkling conviction that he can tell the whole of humanity something fundamental about the way it thinks, and not only that but teach (some might say, betray) this lesson to the machines, is uniquely enthralling—a way-out tabloid story that just might turn out to be true.

"We like to think that we are inscrutable and that the way we reason is a mystical process. That just isn't so. Common sense is composed of a very large, though not infinite, number of facts and rules," says Lenat, who believes in his heart that Cyc can keep track of them all.

The Cyc project is dedicated to the proposition that to have sense you must have knowledge to make sense of. Common sense is built on a foundation of common knowledge, or, as Lenat prefers, "human consensual knowledge," either label referring to the immense store of general information the average person knows. Much of common knowledge is acquired during childhood: water runs downhill; animals live for one solid interval of time; if you smash a wooden table to bits, the pieces are still wood, but are no longer a table; ketchup is not a vegetable; no object can be in two places at once; how to inhale. The no-brainer stuff that encyclopedia editors assume their readers understand and that tabloid editors figure their readers either don't quite grasp or are willing to overlook.

"Perhaps the hardest truth to face, one that AI has been trying to wriggle out of for 34 years, is that there is probably no elegant, effortless way to obtain this immense knowledge base. Rather, the bulk of the effort must (at least initially) be manual entry of assertion after assertion. . . . In short, we must bite the bullet," write Lenat and Cyc project coleader, R. V. Guha.

Just as Denis Diderot led his eighteenth-century team of French scholars in a massive thirty-year project to gather all the Western world's scholarly knowledge into one *Encyclopédie*, Lenat and a dozen researchers (in MCC parlance, knowledge enterers) have set out to summarize contemporary *common* knowledge in their database. Where doesn't one search for the obvious? The amiably motley crew of grad students and post-docs, including a musician, a botanist, a psychologist, an engineer and a cultural anthropologist, has set out to gather up to 100 million rules, facts, tendencies and other assertions from personal experience, periodicals, advertisements, instruction manuals, guidebooks, and wherever other insights about daily life can be gleaned.

The trick is to notice what's being taken for granted. Common knowledge is usually tacit—that is, not summonable upon command, but instead elicited point by picayune point. In reading an automotive manual, a knowledge enterer generally skips right over technical stuff about fuel mixtures and compression ratios, for these are not considered common knowledge but the kind of specialized facts that most people would have to look up.

Instead, the knowledge enterer has the excruciatingly simple-minded task of making sure that Cyc knows the basics: that an automobile has four wheels, is driven by one person at a time, can come in different colors, consumes gasoline and oil—not so much the facts of the text but what it takes to understand those facts. Can't marvel at the antilock brakes without first knowing that under certain driving conditions, automobiles tend to skid. A point I'll keep coming back to throughout this book is that what the average person knows, of course, depends on who and where that average person is.

Sometimes one statement encapsulates a world view: After learning the sentence, "Napoleon died in 1821; Wellington was saddened," Cyc required several months of background and analysis to absorb how a statesman might feel at the demise of his greatest adversary. In assembling such an eclectic knowledge base, the MCC team has had to be opportunistic, borrowing concepts, applications, and whatever else works from such AI luminaries as Marvin Minsky of MIT, John McCarthy and Ed Feigenbaum of Stanford and many others. Lenat is a devout eclectic who preaches that the secret is that there is no secret to understanding our common experience. Common sense slips in and out of theory nets like a handful of eels: no set of equations or neat hypotheses can handle it all. "Ideological blinders have kept AI in the dark for too long. Cyc is a set of partial solutions, the union of which will get us just barely where we need to go," says the avid tinkerer, proud of his "toolkit" approach.

The Cyc team obviously has great affection for their leader with the ten-gallon ego, judging from the jokes and bits of crushed ice flying back and forth at their daily luncheon. It falls to the visitor to tweak the crusaders, a group that, seven years closeknit, seems a bit Holy Grail. I volunteer a definition of common sense that I'd heard the day before: "It takes common sense to be pregnant and raise a family while your husband's off in Saudi [Arabia] with [Operation] Desert Storm," said a young Texas woman, talking of her sister. How would that sit with their fledgling megabrain?

"It's important to distinguish between common sense and common-sense behavior, which is what your friend's assertion sounds like. A simpler example of common-sense behavior is the woman who covers her watch and jewelry when walking down dark city streets," says Lenat, adding that "Common sense used to say that if a watch is broken, the thing to do is take it to the repair shop to get it fixed. But now common sense might say the easier and less-expensive thing to do is discard that watch and get another one." All this information, Lenat assures me by the way, Cyc has known for quite some time.

The Face of Common Sense

When confronted with a homely baby, the parents beaming by, the only decent thing to do, is tell a whopping lie. I am staring into the face of common sense and it is not pretty, I thought but did not say as Lenat and his associate Karen Pittman proudly presented Cyc's superwide terminal, with so many windows popping in and out that it looked like a great computerized fly with rectangular eyes all over its face. Computers cannot see, I reminded myself, as Pittman patiently explained the beauty beneath the screen.

Cyc's basic unit of knowledge is called just that, a *unit,* which can be either a tangible thing or a concept. Knowledge about a unit is stored in a *frame,* the rectangles in question. A frame is essentially an electronic index card filled with definitions and description statements about its unit. The frame for the unit "Person" includes these definitions: HumanScaleObject, LegalEntity, SentientAnimal, and BiologicalLivingObject.

(LoveMachine apparently does not make the grade.) Descriptive statements, which heavily outnumber the definitions, are arranged in categories, with specific values filled in. Thus for the "Person" frame, the category "Performsdaily" includes such values as "TakingANight'sSleep," "TeethCleaning," and so on.

Clustered with the "Person" frame would be other frames such as "DouglasLenat" and "MaryShepherd" (Cyc's administrative director). Frames that are conceptually related are called *sibs,* short for siblings. All sibs describing human beings (rather than, say, automobiles or planets), simply list "Person" among their definition statements, rather than listing all the same personhood attributes over again in each frame. Thus, once Cyc reads that "Douglas Lenat" is a person, all the other definitions and descriptions of personhood automatically accrue to him. The sib structure makes adding new frames much easier. If Cyc already knows "House" and "Garage," it takes only a few alterations to add "Barn."

What if Mary skips a night's sleep every now and then, or Douglas forgets to brush his teeth? Could Cyc live with the contradictions? In life and in Cyc, rules are made to be broken. About 95 percent of Cyc's knowledge is entered in the form of default logic, meaning that Cyc assumes a statement is usually true, although there may be exceptions. Cyc has learned that "Birds usually fly," except that some birds can't fly if they are dead, trapped, penguins, and so on. (Oddly, the formulation "birds usually fly," which is a verbatim transcription of the rule, is incorrect in most instances. Birds usually are able to fly but of course, they are not airborne most of the time.) Similarly, the proposition that "If something is not supported, then it falls," is true in most cases, except for helium-filled balloons, space objects, and (most) birds.

To illustrate the value of default logic, Lenat uses the example of assuming that one's car stays where it has been parked. "Your car may have just been stolen, but it's better to get an occasional surprise than to exhibit the irrational behavior that would result from always thinking that your car was stolen." Many rules are true in life but not fiction.

Simple default reasoning is standard in AI. Lenat and Guha have expanded the true-or-not concept by creating a way to ask "true in what context?" Cyc's most powerful unit of inference is called the "microtheory," a general statement that is true in a given set of contexts. For example, having learned that "Nothing can be older than its creator," the program can also extend this reasoning to a variety of contexts, concluding that no painting can be older than its artist, no car older than the company, or the factory, that produced it, that no child can be older than its parent.

Cyc is programmed to assume a general context of rationality. The microtheory that "Owning an object is a necessary pre-condition to consuming it," assumes a calm, law-abiding state of affairs—responsible parties in a setting where the usual laws of ownership and private property prevail. At this writing, Bosnia, Somalia, Liberia, Cambodia and many other areas of the world would not qualify as such contexts. Similarly, the microtheory that "After the sale, the buyer owns the object," might not al-ways hold true in lawless or volatile contexts, like a drug deal where bad guys take the money, and then the drugs back too.

Similarly, the computer is inclined to assume that actions are accompanied by rational motivations, that the buyer needs the object bought, and that the seller needs the money. But "If the seller was engaging in the event for spite (e.g. a dying man selling his house for a dollar so that his children didn't get it), or if the buyer were engaging in this action as an act of charity, most of the axioms . . . would be inapplicable to this case. It is not as though the individual rules in the theory are defaults and these cases are exceptions to these rules: These cases are simply beyond the scope of the theory," writes Guha, who is working to program Cyc to accommodate these special cases.

Microtheories enable Cyc to overlook the irrelevant, programming it with biases that mirror our own. Perhaps the most important of these is a causal bias, meaning that explanations of cause and effect are preferred to those which are simply descriptive. If Cyc were asked to interpret a situation where a window was broken, and a rock was sitting on the floor, Cyc would deduce that the rock had come through the window, rather than, say, simply concluding that the rock had always been sitting there, and the window had always been broken. (Interestingly, this may be a Western bias. Studies of schoolchildren's interpretations of photographs of this rock-through-the-window scene found that children from Japan, and particularly China, were more likely to describe the scene in current, static detail rather than attributing causality, as the American children were inclined to do.)

A minor ideological difference between Lenat and Roger Schank, a natural-language expert at Northwestern University, gives an inkling of the different learning needs of Cyc's mind and that of a person, particularly a child. In his recent book, *Tell Me a Story,* Schank argues that experience, stored in the form of stories, is the most important form of knowledge. But Lenat counters that you don't need a story to know enough not to drive the wrong way up an exit ramp. You don't need ever to have done it, or even ever to have heard about anyone who has done it, to realize the importance of avoiding the head-on collision that might occur. Schank might counter that stories of head-on collisions are the key to understanding the ramp's

specific importance, but for Lenat, the logic of two cars collid-
ing head-on at full speed amply suffices. Wisely, Lenat's dis-
agreement with Schank's emphasis on the primacy of stories
doesn't keep him from using them when appropriate: "The first
time going out on a date is a rich experience best shared through
a story."

Who is right in this little dispute depends on whether the
student is a person or a machine. Though we can make a point
with logic only, a story may be the only or best way to drive the
lesson home. Take learning the rule that says to look out for
traffic before crossing the street. Cyc absorbs the rule with emo-
tionless precision, and has no need for dramatic iteration. But
even if a child were clearly instructed in street-crossing procedures, and understood them every bit as well as Cyc, a story
might still be necessary or helpful. This is not a question of
logical understanding, because a child who foolishly runs out
into the street might nonetheless have responded correctly
about looking for traffic if asked by an adult or questioned on a
school test—that is, given the same chance to reflect that Cyc
would have if asked. Yet behavior that might at first seem comparative human inefficiency is actually something else altogether, considering the different needs of the two minds. The
function of a story, say, about the little boy who got run over—
and couldn't go out and play for a whole year!—is to embed
that rule deeper than logic, down to the level of reflex. Human
common sense must not only say you don't go running into the
street, it must also produce the appropriate safe behavior. That's
a level of understanding forever unknown and unnecessary to
Cyc, which cannot move an inch.

Perhaps the eeriest Cyc-ic phenomenon is the program's tendency to muse and cogitate late at night, after the knowledge
enterers have gone home. As you fall asleep thinking about

something and wake up the next morning with the answer, Cyc spends the night roaming through its memory banks, looking for associations, analogies, contradictions, and so on. The most important function of this soul searching is to identify inconsistencies that might cause "divergence," the dreaded "endless-loop" scenario that Cyc might, like a paranoid obsessed with the conundrum "Everything I say is a lie," squander its energy trying to reconcile some inconsistency, and crash. If "mother" were defined by one knowledge enterer as "female parent" and another as "bearer of child," Cyc could be launched on the path of perdition. But by identifying the contradiction in a nighttime analogy hunt, and displaying it as a question for the knowledge enterers to answer next morning, Lenat hopes that Cyc can avoid divergence.

Nighttime discoveries are also made by comparing frames for similarities. Among sibs, Cyc might surmise that DouglasLenat and MaryShepherd know each other because they live in the same city, work at the same company, and so on. Another analogy that Cyc found significant was that USA and United States of America seemed to be related. (Cyc had to be specifically instructed that the two items in question are not only analogous, but synonymous.) Every now and then comes the existential leap: Upon learning the microtheory that "Like associates with like"—that children tend to know other children, scientists other scientists—and then upon learning that Mary Shepherd likes Cyc, the machine wondered: "Am I a person, or is Mary Shepherd a computer program?"

The Good Soldier Cyc

In spring 1991, MCC gave a demonstration of how Cyc could be helpful in marketing automobiles. Participants in the test project filled out questionnaires on their occupation, age, location, family status, hobbies, self-image and many other attributes. Cyc proceeded to draw inferences about the buyers and the sort of cars and features they would desire. A single person living alone might want a small car but not, Cyc reasoned, if she were a real estate agent, where a more luxurious four- or five-seater would be more suitable. A boating enthusiast might need a more powerful vehicle to pull his craft but an avid skier would appreciate nonskid antilock brakes for those trips to snow country. Someone who has eleven children might require a van unless, Cyc observed, that someone was twenty-one years old. Why? Because twenty-one year-old persons rarely if ever have that many children. Cyc used its common sense to conclude that there had been a mistaken entry, a typo made when the customer meant to enter one child but hit the "1" key twice. All in all, a tour de force of practical reasoning.

But is it common sense? Not according to John Searle, a cognitive philosopher at Berkeley. In his infamous "Chinese Room" analogy, Searle likens the performance of supposedly intelligent computer programs to a person who does not speak Chinese but who sits alone in a room with Chinese dictionaries and reference works. In Searle's scenario, Cyc answering questions about which automobile to buy is like the person in the room responding to inquiries written in Chinese that have been slipped under the door. The ignorant but diligent person then uses the dictionaries to translate the question, do some research and compose the response. Thus the semblance of intelligence is created without true understanding, according to Searle, even if the answers turn out to be every bit as good as those which would be given by a native Chinese speaker who really understood what was going on.

Frankly, this argument is aggressively ignorant of what real translation entails. Anyone who has tried to steer through a foreign country with dictionary in hand knows that. Yet Searle's Chinese Room scenario is good in the way that an annoying television commercial must be conceded effective if it injects the message into your mind.

Tufts University cognitive philosopher Daniel C. Dennett is the most recent among many to try scrubbing out Searle's semantic stain. In his widely regarded *Consciousness Explained* (1992), Dennett writes, "The fact is that any program that could actually hold up its end in the conversation depicted [in Searle's Chinese Room scenario] would have to be an extraordinarily supple, sophisticated, and multilayered system, brimming with 'world knowledge' and meta-knowledge and meta-meta-knowledge about its own responses, the likely responses of its interlocutor, its own 'motivations' and the motivations of its interlocutor, and much, much more." All in all, not a bad description of Cyc.

But what about oval door handles? Buying a car is every bit as emotional and impressionistic as it is a rational assessment of one's realistic needs. True, the Cyc automobile demonstration included questions designed to elicit information about prospective consumers' self-image, but compared to the hound-dog instincts of a hungry salesman, this Q-and-A bit is greasy kid's stuff. You know those Infiniti Q-45s, with the oval-within-oval door handles? They are sooo slick, the way the elliptical shape mirrors the curves of the car! Yet the last thing any wary customer is going to do is tell some computer program about this totally irrational weakness for some luxury feature. But a good salesperson watches the way prospective customers look at a car, what they wander back to, run their fingers over, point out to their friends. To them, it's only common sense that people never tell you everything you need to know.

The question is, can common sense exist without senses? The Cyc project finds itself in the semantically dubious position of pretending to common sense without affording its program any sensory mechanisms. Except for some very limited optical scanning ability to absorb printed information, MCC's knowledge enterers are the closest thing to being Cyc's eyes and ears, and even then incidentally, for sensory simulation is far from their primary role. Can second-hand data adequately substitute for the direct and indivisible link between sensing the world and at the same moment understanding what one sees, hears, tastes, touches and feels?

In a great *Star Trek* episode, "Spock's Brain," aliens stole Mr. Spock's brain, put it in a life-support machine and let it run their civilization. The aliens provided the data and Spock's brain made the decisions, not unlike the relationship between Cyc and its human inputters. The measure of plausibility in science fiction is whether or not something is theoretically possible, which the story of Spock's brain, and of Cyc, seem to be.

Theoretical possibilities frequently work out to be practical impossibilities, and even a devout AI adherent such as Dennett begs off on the proposition that the mind can function independently of its senses. In fact, Dennett opens *Consciousness Explained* with a discussion of the "brain in a vat," a situation analogous to the predicament of both Spock and Cyc. He proceeds to trash what he considers to be an "old saw" of skeptical philosophy dating from the days of René Descartes, the seventeenth-century founder of modern philosophy. Descartes held that evil demons could be tricking and subverting humankind's imperfect senses, and that we could all, in effect, be nothing more than brains in vats systematically deceived into believing that we are experiencing physical reality. But Dennett rebuts powerfully that such fakery is impossible, if not in hypothetical principle then in practical fact:

Throw a skeptic a dubious coin, and in a second or two of hefting, scratching, ringing, tasting, and just plain looking at how the sun glints on its surface, the skeptic will consume more bits of information than a Cray supercomputer can organize in a year. Making a *real* but counterfeit coin is child's play; making a *simulated* coin out of nothing but organized nerve stimulations (as would be necessary to trick an envatted brain) is beyond human technology now and probably forever [italics his].

Still, good judgment doesn't necessarily depend on having sound physical senses. Helen Keller proved that. What the woman who could not see, hear, or talk lacked in perceptual abilities she more than made up for by her determination to know about the world and desire to express herself. Most of her learning about the world came not as a result of direct perception but from interpretations by others—her teacher, her parents, the authors of the books she read. Of course, curiosity and desire are emotions as alien to Cyc as they are to an encyclopedia sitting on the shelf. Yet with programmatic persistence Cyc also learns from the secondhand interpretations of its human tutors and from its growing ability to read.

Can This Encyclopedia Read?

By the time Cyc is completed, the program will require the equivalent of 3,000 to 4,000 one-megabyte computer disks. If built with standard Tinkertoy parts, the brain would fill up the better part of the Houston Astrodome. All to hold the common knowledge that most of us take for granted . . . slips our mind. So what makes Cyc anything more than just a giant $35-million encyclopedia of the everyday data that, after all, none of us human beings really need to look up?

The MCC project has a few raw nerves, and comparing Cyc to an encyclopedia is the way to stick one of them: "One of the unfortunate myths about Cyc is that its aim is to be a sort of electronic encyclopedia, . . . If anything Cyc is the complement of an encyclopedia," write Lenat and Guha. By insisting that the human mind is *not* essentially encyclopedic, and that neither is Cyc, Lenat backpedals from the eminently graspable mind-as-encyclopedia metaphor that did, after all, give his brainchild its name. He also rejects the thinking of an esteemed former colleague, Herbert A. Simon of Carnegie-Mellon, who does believe that the mind *is* like "a big, indexed encyclopedia." Simon, the recipient of the 1978 Nobel Memorial Prize in Economics and the 1986 National Science Medal, takes special delight in making our species feel less than unique. He recently told *The New York Times:* "To those who would say there is something special about creativity, I would say, 'Look at the evidence,' " . . . making new discoveries "is a matter of having good reasoning processes, having the right encyclopedia knowledge, having the right motivations and living at the right time."

But how many encyclopedias know how to read? Lenat and Guha contend, "The aim is that one day Cyc ought to contain enough common-sense knowledge to . . . read through and assimilate any encyclopedia article, that is, to be able to answer the sorts of questions that you or I could after having just read any article, questions that neither you nor Cyc could be expected to answer beforehand." The part about Cyc reading, however, is the other raw nerve. It turns out that Lenat made a whopper of a promise to get the project going. For Cyc to gather anywhere near the common knowledge base it needs, the machine has to learn to start reading on its own, and at computer hyperspeed. But in order to read, Cyc must first have the knowledge to understand what it's reading. A programmer's version of *Catch-22*.

Slowing everything down is the necessity of translating virtually all of Cyc's input into CycL, a symbolic machine language derived from the main AI language, Lisp. Thus the statement "Birds usually fly" is translated by the knowledge enterer into **isa(xBird)/\#abl(x)›flies(x),** which then is keyboarded into the Cyc program. This "manual insertion" is painstakingly slow, and as of this writing, about 80 percent through the project's time span, only 1.5 million assertions, or 1.5 percent of the 100 million estimated to be necessary, have been entered.

By 1995, Lenat firmly contends, Cyc will be absorbing 50 percent of its new information directly from natural-language texts—that is, without manual translation. Knowledge enterers will gradually be replaced by "tutors" standing by to answer the computer's questions. But what will Cyc actually *be able* to read? Natural language is flavored with irony, wordplay, double entendres and other figures of speech. Like an infant being weaned from formula to solids, Cyc will start on a very restricted diet: encyclopedia articles, handbook instructions, how-to guides, and other clearcut, straightforward material. It will be a long time, if ever, before Cyc can stomach spicy, rich dishes like good steamy novels and the junk food sold in supermarket tabloids, without help from the tutors.

Elaine Rich, an MCC researcher working on Cyc's natural-language interface, explains that there are two basic challenges to reading natural language: (1) understanding what is written, and (2) determining its validity. She illustrates with this example: Let's say we are told, "George is a fire engine." If we were sitting with a kindergarten class, we might expect a story about a fire engine named George, maybe the cousin of the "little engine that could." But in most instances we would take this statement as an implied simile, a figurative analogy for George's personality and temperament. Maybe we know George, and don't think he's a fire engine at all. No, on balance we'd say that George is a doormat, and a pinhead. Imagine Cyc's problems trying to digest this simile! George, Cyc might be forced to conclude, is really a pain in the gut.

Lots of useful hints can be gleaned from syntactical context. In the sentence, "George jabwocked Nancy," we know that George did something to Nancy even if we haven't an inkling of what the word "jabwocked" means. Of course, we may have some inkling, because the verb sounds as if it comes from Lewis Carroll's "Jabberwocky," a poem that takes brilliant advantage of our ability to infer meaning from syntax. But even without catching the literary reference, Cyc would understand that George performed some action on Nancy, and it could do so even if still confused about George's true "fire-engine" nature.

Metonymy, the natural-language rule that anything can stand for anything else as long as people can be reasonably expected to understand it, is another big problem for Cyc. When the newspaper says that "Moscow asks Washington," it's obvious to us that the reporter does not mean that the whole population of the Russian capital spoke up in unison to the residents of Washington. Rich reports some success in this area. For example, Cyc is now able to comprehend that the statement, "I love to listen to Bach," refers to the composer's music, not to the (dead) man himself. Cyc also makes the same assumption that most of us do, namely that the Bach in question is Johann Sebastian, rather than any of his children who also composed music.

Recent brain-scan studies indicate that when processing natural language, the cerebrum draws simultaneously on several discrete centers, including one for vocabulary and one for grammar. Cyc creates the equivalent of a grammar center by converting all its CycL input into an even more arcane dialect, CycL Heuristic, an internal machine language specially designed to process the rules of grammar, rhetoric, and so on. Here the machine has a distinct advantage over its human counterpart. According to Helen Neville of the Salk Institute, the brain's vocabulary center has the capacity to expand throughout life, but the grammar center usually stops growing during adolescence. That's one reason why children have an easier time than adults in learning new languages. Cyc, by contrast, has no inherent age limitation to its acquisition of grammatical knowledge.

Beyond rules and figures of speech, learning to read entails assessing context, a much more intricate and implicit reading skill. Just as children eventually catch on that the declarations made in advertisements have a different, usually lesser, truth value than those made in their textbooks, and that there is another whole category of truth for the religious materials they read, Cyc must also learn appropriate levels of doubt and gauge the importance of factual accuracy in determining the truth of what it reads. Because Lenat holds up the supermarket tabloids as a standard of absurdity, a clarion extreme, I thought it might be interesting to examine how even this far-less-than-subtle medium might cause Cyc some confusion:

GEORGE BUSH IN NUDE ROMP WITH ALL-MALE GROUP OF COMMUNIST SYMPATHIZERS WHO BEAT HIM FOR PLEASURE!

"What an experience!" exclaimed Bush, fondly recalling the bizarre 1983 encounter that occurred while he was Vice President of the United States. "It will be in my memory until I die!"

For the record, all facts and quotations about the then Vice President George Bush referred to in this section are technically accurate and completely verifiable. Nothing is made up. But whatever the technicalities, common sense says this story is essentially false. In other words, there's got to be a catch.

How do we know that? How can most of us tell right off the bat that the Bush story above is full of beans? Do we have common-sense "catch catchers" that beep like price scanners whenever something nonsensical is run by them? As explored in the next chapter, our common-sense view of the world develops throughout childhood in a fairly predictable and standardized progression. Therefore, shouldn't it operate in adults in fairly predictable, standardized ways? And if common sense is what everyone agrees upon, doesn't logic suggest that we all reach that agreement through the same fundamental reasoning processes?

Yet another paradox of common sense for Cyc to consider is that although it does lead people with widely different perspectives to the same conclusions—all roads do lead to Rome—there is no Appian Way; each individual gets there by his, her or its own route. The lady next to us in line smoothing out her *Cream of Wheat* coupons knows perfectly well that nice people don't do things like what those headlines say, and that President Bush always seemed quite the fine gentleman to her. Her patriotic husband accepts without questioning that presidents of the United States do not romp naked with communists, period. Though the loyal Republicans stuck behind us might not be too sure about certain, shall we say, loose-zippered Democrats, they are right as rain that "Family Values" George is not the kind to get involved in that kind of hanky-panky.

George Bush's friends and supporters wouldn't give the story a third thought: if nothing else, the former CIA director is far too clever to get caught with his pants down, much less be quoted as loving it. Gossip junkies and liberals reeling from twelve years of Reagan/Bush/Quayle might have crossed their fingers and hoped for the best, but they knew intuitively that this scandal was just too good to be true. Plus endless permutations and combinations thereof, all leading to the same thumbs-down verdict.

Like a heat-seeking missile, common sense has a nose for the truth, wherever it's fired from. In fact, common sense can even be right for the wrong reasons. Many of us would dismiss the Bush story simply on the assumption that whatever tabloids print is utter nonsense. But publications such as *The National Enquirer* and *Weekly World News* are multimillion-dollar enterprises represented by high-priced attorneys whose job it is to avoid major lawsuits by practicing the art of the permissible lie—that is, lies that can be gotten away with. Stories such as the Bush tale above are dangerous to run without a redeeming grain of truth, which, after all, is an absolute defense against libel under American law.

Here is Vice President George Bush's handwritten note from 1983, quoted in its entirety, addressed to and still hanging in the Finnish Sauna Society in Helsinki:

> Thank you for taking away from your precious Saturday to give so generously to me and my friends. The true sauna will be in my memory until I die.
>
> What an experience!
>
> > Gratefully,
> > George Bush

The "true sauna," according to Pirkko Valtakari, the Helsinki society's executive director, is unisex except if within the family, naked without bathing suits or any other covering, and usually includes beating oneself and/or others with birch branches and splashing water on hot rocks to sizzle the steam. Then a plunge into the icy-cold lake outside, back in for a beverage that should not be but often is alcoholic, and then, very important, repeat the whole procedure all over again. And when Bush visited Finland in 1983, the country was still "Finlandized," under Soviet economic and political domination, meaning that in all likelihood the vice president was sweating with some buck-naked socialists, at the very least.

"So what if natural language [reading capability] takes twenty years, so long as it is done," declares Minsky, who isn't writing the checks. But for Lenat, who isn't writing them either, the day of reckoning is approaching a little too fast. Recently his original prediction that "no one would ever dream of owning a computer without Cyc" was pushed back from "turn of the century" to 2015. And like a politician whose campaign promises are coming due, Lenat now claims that project will be a success even if Cyc research simply provides "some insights into issues involved in building large common-sense knowledge bases." That's the CS survival skill known as strategic retreat.

By the time Douglas Lenat was four years old, he was already manipulating other people's minds. That was the age when he wrote "How to Handle Your Parents." The little book included strategies on how to get your parents to stop fighting—ask Mom, "Don't you love Dad?" and vice versa. This opus upset his mother when she first saw it and also twenty years later, when she found it in the attic, reread it, and threw it into the trash. That boy had figured out something he wasn't supposed to know and had set it down for the world to see.

Lenat's clever strategy of asking first one parent, then the other whether they loved each other is a gem of common sense, an inspired practical solution to an important problem. And it suggests a simple standard of judgment for his machine: will Cyc ever have as much common sense as Lenat did when he was four years old?

3

Where Does Common Sense Come From?

What's Plain Before Your Face

It was getting on toward midnight and the F train had just pulled into the Jay Street subway station in Brooklyn. Into our car strode a tall African-American woman, around thirty years old, stylishly dressed in brown leather and tan gabardine, with a boy of no more than four. For a long moment she surveyed the homebound stragglers and then in a clear, sober voice announced that as of that moment she and her son were resigning from the black race. The woman then proceeded to spew the vilest stream of anti-black nonsense I'd ever heard. It was like the KKK's David Duke on pentothal, like the demon from *The Exorcist* vomiting pea soup right into the black passengers' faces.

Common sense says avoid ugliness (especially when it's coming at you live). Turn away and hunker down was the general reflex in the subway car that night. Night students dived back into their nursing manuals, law-school textbooks, racing forms, even litter on the floor as long as it was readable. Someone homeless, a man judging from the form, who was lying nose-in on a banquette of three seats, snuggled in even deeper. A trio, maybe brothers, probably Russian, pretended not to catch on and continued sounding out the English in the Dr. M. D. Tusch ads: "Hemorr-hoids, Fissures, An-al Warts." An actress-waitress-dancer dog tired from some Greenwich Village late shift anxiously scanned her *Backstage* classifieds for escape routes, then dissolved into her personal stereo set.

The little boy, handsome in his blue suit, red bow tie, and shiny black shoes, made total avoidance impossible, or at least unseemly. He ran up to each of his mommy's victims, shouting "Fuck you! Fuck you!" in the cutest little voice you ever heard. He took a fit and shook his head so hard that it seemed he was trying to spring something loose inside. But when his mother turned her attack to black children, how they can't read, can't compete with the Asians, can't do shit, her exceptional son ran right over to the homeless man and taunted the poor fellow like a chihuahua yap-yapping at a German shepherd that could not or would not rouse itself. I think it was the first time any of us had ever looked upon a four-year-old with fear.

Like gravity, common sense is much more noticeable in its absence than its presence, a mysterious force essential to the natural order of things. Somehow the little boy in the bow tie, a grotesque caricature of Louis Farakkhan and the black pride that his Nation of Islam so vehemently preaches, had managed to switch our gravity off that night. Rattling along on the F-train, racism twisting into self-hatred like a snake eating its tail, was like bouncing along the dark side of the moon. The guy sitting next to me, about my age, my ilk, was reading *The Sound and the Fury* for dear life. Finally the whole scene got to him and he lowered the book, turned to me, and said: "Faulkner could have dealt with these people. But frankly, I can't."

A knot of us escaped at the Seventh Avenue stop and in complete complicity, though without word or glance exchanged, walked together along the main commercial drag of Park Slope. It was great to be back on home turf, where things "make sense." The hysterical display of twenty minutes earlier was not necessarily a symptom of anything deeper, I assured myself. It was simply an isolated incident, nothing more than that. To generalize from a particular, no matter how poignant, is, after all, to sin against logic. What about the millions and millions of little boys and girls safe at home at that midnight hour, snug in bed and identity? Therefore nothing can be confidently inferred, I hoped, about the state of the world, America, New York, or even the F-train, which happens to be one of my city's finest lines, from this one little subterranean psychodrama.

In George Orwell's *1984,* Big Brother reduced the chocolate ration and then had demonstrations organized to thank Him for *raising* the chocolate ration. Every bit as palpable a contradiction as the little boy being taught to despise people because of their skin color even though that color was his own. One would think so glaring an inconsistency at such a tender age would impair a child's ability to function. Yet that boy was anything but stupid—positively clever at knowing whom to taunt and when, particularly in guessing that the covered-up homeless person was black—a solid assumption, from what he had been taught. All in all, a good little helper to his mom. If that child had a candy bar and you took away half, no way would he thank you for it.

Watching a little boy and his mother defiantly proclaim their self-hatred to the insensate subway crowd can make even the simple belief that common sense exists at all seem hopelessly naive. Maybe his being very young, not much more than a toddler, somehow protected him from the absurd contradiction. But what if that child were, say, five or six instead of three or four? Would the wedge driven between him and the facts be splitting harder wood?

Hard-Wired or Acquired?

For narrative convenience and in hope of good luck, I have named that boy Tyrone, after a childhood friend whom I have always admired.

Odd to think that troubled little Tyrone probably has more common sense than Cyc ever will, even with Lenat and his team of knowledge-enterers teaching their supercomputer whatever it needs to know. Cyc, if it is fed too much incorrect or contradictory information, may become confused, can even collapse. Yet Tyrone seems capable of remaining functionally astute even while fundamentally confused. Why such a disparity between the two minds? Is the human brain so much more powerful and supple in its ability to acquire knowledge and make judgments? Or do we have a built-in head start over the computer? In other words, does common sense come hard-wired in human beings?

Current scholarly wisdom concurs with what proud parents have intuited for millennia—that infants are born understanding much more than they can communicate. Far from being the *tabula rasa* or mental blank slate that John Locke and other empirical philosophers long supposed the newborn, "the mind of the neonate is highly organized to process incoming sensory experience in certain ways. Newborn infants can visually recognize the real shape of a rectangle at various orientations . . . recognize human faces and their mother's voice. At the very beginning of its life, the newborn infant mentally represents aspects of its environment," writes University of Toronto philosopher-psychologist Lynd Forguson in *Common Sense (1989)*, an insightful scholarly text in which he synthesizes current and historical research (pp. 48–49).

Jean Piaget was among the first to spot the resemblance between the *tabula rasa* theory and a very full diaper. After years of playing with, talking to, and designing simple experiments to understand very young children, the great Swiss psychologist discovered that cognitive development proceeds in genetically predetermined stages, following much the same sequence in everyone. In other words, we are all born with developmental instructions that are carried out in due time. Although programmed commands may not be common sense itself, because the decision making is not fully conscious, neither is this the total mental blankness or abject receptivity that philosophers—who had never made it a practice to actually work with the youngsters about whom they theorized—assumed.

Unfortunately, Piaget erred in his belief that very young children reason quite differently than adults, and that they are often incapable of understanding logic. Scholars now agree that Piaget overestimated the children's language skills, and therefore underestimated their intellectual sophistication. (Anyone who has traveled to a region where the language and customs are strange might have conveyed a similarly out-of-it impression.)

The language barrier to cognitive study has been broken by an experimental method known as the looking-time procedure, which assumes that infants, much like adults, will look markedly longer at new or surprising stimuli than at familiar or expected stuff. Two-and-a-half-month-olds demonstrate, by the duration of their puzzled stares, the very commonsensical conclusion that a foam rubber ball should not be able to roll through a wooden box. Five-month-olds ponder longer at surprising arithmetic results—when one Mickey Mouse doll and then a second doll are each placed behind a screen, but yield, when the screen is lowered, say, three Mickeys rather than the expected two.

The simplest assumption, according to Karen Wynn, the University of Arizona developmental psychologist whose

experiments have demonstrated infants' quantitative abilities, is
that "human beings are innately endowed with certain mental
mechanisms . . . already operating unconsciously in infants."
That is, we are born with them. She adds, "The business of
psychology is to specify the principles that underlie common
sense, and not just take it at face value. When we say, 'it's just
common sense,' that usually means there's actually something
very interesting going on. The human mind is allowing something to be privileged over some other thing for no logical
reason."

Survival instincts are the prelinguistic core of common-sense
reasoning; nothing is more sensible than doing what one must
to survive. Wynn cites the example of getting out of the way
when a bus is bearing down, and points out that this sort of
survival instinct is present in very young infants. In one experiment, three-month-olds are seated on a table minding their own
business, when all of a sudden a big pillow in the shape of a cube
is shoved rapidly toward them by a hidden "researcher" pushing
a rod. Babies seeing the large cube bearing down on them become frightened and demonstrate the same startle-flight response
that a pedestrian might when confronted with oncoming traffic. (Effects of this response upon the researchers can only be
conjectured.)

Perhaps the best-known demonstration of infants' survival
instinct is the visual cliff, in which six- to nine-month-old infants
routinely decline to crawl from the edge of a table onto an in-
visible glass surface, even when lovingly encouraged by their
parents. Some cite this as an example of inherent common sense
(in the children, that is), although newborn chicks and other
animals born or hatched with the ability to self-locomote also
avoid the cliff, indicating that such risk reluctance may be auto-
matic and unconscious. Sad to consider that as a six-month-old

infant Tyrone would have resolutely declined to cross the visual cliff but might now consider jumping onto the subway tracks if that served his mother's needs.

Today the value of the newborn's mind is being bid up and up like a sleeper stock pounced on by Wall Street, with no selloff in sight. The next scientific frontier is the in-utero world. Where does that idyllic introduction to life fit into the heredity versus environment scheme? Anecdotal evidence continues to pile up that daily reading, singing and otherwise stimulating the fetus in the womb can eventually contribute to the child's development. Already, French researchers have used hydrophones to determine that the maturing fetus can sense vibrations from music and other sounds in the mother's surroundings. At this writing the expected repeal of the ban on experiments using fetal tissue may eventually lead to advances in our knowledge, though perhaps at some ineffably indecent expense. Whatever the methods, the real breakthroughs will come as researchers learn to shift their perspective, and figure out the common-sense rules of the womb.

Opening the Mind's Eye

Imagine going back and asking everyone on the F-train with Tyrone that night to recount what had transpired. Their recollections might differ dramatically, and could well be distorted by prejudice and fear. How many would remember the homeless man as black, though we never saw his skin? Or would reject the description, accurate though it was, of mother and child as sober and neatly dressed? Or would deny that anything out of the ordinary happened at all?

In essence, the kind of confusion that we normally associate with trying to describe events in retrospect is, in the opinion of scholars from the ancient Greeks on down, a danger to our perception all the time. Amid the constant barrage of diffuse and elusive impressions, how do we all manage to agree on as much as we do? Does the brain have some special structure or mechanism which standardizes this torrent of input—which helps put the "common" in common sense?

Ironically, the further contemporary psychology moves toward the notion of an innate common sense that we all share, the closer it comes to some very ancient beliefs.

Aristotle thought of common sense as a discrete bodily faculty, a sixth sense that culminated the other five. Its role was to coordinate data on sight, hearing, smell, taste and touch, thus enabling the mind to apprehend the "common sensibles," qualities such as motion, volume and shape that might be perceived by more than one faculty. In Aristotle's psychology, if it looks like a duck, quacks like a duck, and walks like a duck, it's the common sense that pulls all these inputs together so that each person's mind can go ahead and declare that it is a duck.

Because you can't have a sense without an organ to produce it, Aristotle speculated that such an organ might be located in the heart. (Hence the expression "to learn by heart," forms of which are still found in many languages.) But over the centuries the common-sense organ atrophied until René Descartes declared that it was alive and well and living in the brain. Descartes believed that the pineal gland, a baby pea-sized nodule that sits on the midline of the brain—making it the only organ directly connected to the central nervous system rather than paired with either hemisphere—was the brain's central-processing station for sensory input. (We are still not sure of the pineal's function, though current best guesses give it a sexual, rather than sensory, role.)

Suspicious that the bodily senses are flawed and untrustworthy, the French skeptic theorized that people could not agree on the basic facts of existence and share a general perception of reality without some sort of universal translator between the material world "out there" and the human mind "in here."

Today, psychologists regard this "mind's eye" that sorts through sensory input as a universal ability that unfolds in genetically determined stages—less an organ than a preordained process. According to Forguson, developing the common sense necessary to arrive at a coherent and conventional grasp of reality first requires knowing the difference between the real and the make-believe. This distinction entails the ability to think about what one is thinking, and about what one has thought, which is known as metacognition. Keeping thoughts straight frequently entails making pictures in one's mind, called mental representations, and then thinking about the pictures, a procedure known as metarepresentation.

A tall order, all this thinking about thinking and seeing, yet eighteen months is the age when children begin to engage in pretense and to recognize pretense in others; when a child may happily make believe that a book is a sandwich, or, the example Forguson cites, that a banana is a telephone. And without confusion: a child of a year and a half or so is normally quite capable of first talking into, then taking a bite out of said banana, and going along if Daddy does the same. A few months later, children come to understand the opposite of make-believe: they know that something's strange when a banana starts talking, if a man tries to take a bite out of a real telephone, or if the sofa starts tiptoeing across the room. (Unless, of course, these things happen on television, which very young children accept right off as its own different world.) By around age two, children get the feel of emotional make-believe, when they pretend to have feelings they really don't have: the book/sandwich tasted good, or the message on the banana/telephone was sad.

"In fact, the onset of pretence can usefully be interpreted as the beginning of a child's recognition of symbols: things that can be used to stand for, refer to, that is, represent other things or situations," writes Forguson.

Maybe Tyrone and his mother were playing an elaborate emotional make-believe, a super banana-telephone game that only the two of them really understood. But is this interplay symbolic, or pathetic?

Psychologists take pain to stress the universality of the results they report, and although it is quite true that researchers choose normal, neutral experimental milieus to keep their results un-biased, even that supposed neutrality shows bias. What propor-tion of the world's children live in homes without telephones, or without bananas to use as props in games? If a three-year-old in sub-Saharan Africa desperately pretends that a stick is a nice, ripe banana, or when her counterpart in the perpetually dissolv-ing Yugoslavia patiently dials the wall, is that act bolstering their imagination, destroying their common sense, or both?

When children are forced to use their imagination to repel insane surroundings (as they must in so many parts of the world), or to deny basic personal truths, as little Tyrone particularly did, symbols become desperate alternatives to reality, not just useful representations of it. An important distinction separates make-believe for the fun of it from pretense that is a defense against the world. Yet though it's tempting to conclude that children forced by inhuman circumstances to retreat into their fantasy worlds are therefore somehow common-sense–impaired, it often seems that adults who come from such embattled back-grounds have a *firmer* grasp of reality than those of us who didn't have to fight so hard. Common sense says that even young children can understand the difference between playing games and playing for keeps. Up to a point short of permanent trauma, some mental facility may be gained by sometimes *having* to pretend, rather than simply choosing to.

The Other Point of View

Seeing the world through someone else's eyes, thinking as another person might think, is a cognitive art that takes a lifetime to master. No one has the perfect gift, as Robert Burns put it, "to see ourselves as others see us." Yet the rudimentary understanding that not everyone looks at things the same way we do is essential to getting along in daily life. In Forguson's nutshell definition, a common-sense view of the world comes with realizing that, "People act as they do because of what they desire and what they believe." Not, he might add, because of what *we* desire and *we* believe.

An interesting experiment conducted by psychologists H. Wimmer, J. Perner and their associates, examines the developmental transition from egocentricity to broader perspective. Before an audience of young children, a puppet exhibits a piece of chocolate, places it into the top drawer of a chest, then leaves. While the puppet is offstage and presumably out of sight, the experimenter, in full view of the audience, switches the piece of chocolate to the bottom drawer. The children are asked in which drawer the puppet will look when she returns. The psychologists found that three-year-olds believe the puppet will look into the lower drawer, reasoning that's where the chocolate is now, so that's where the puppet will think it is. They know where the candy is, so why shouldn't the puppet? However, most four-year-olds have developed the ability to think from someone else's perspective and know that the puppet will look for the candy in the drawer where she left it.

If children were little biological robots marching, unless defective, toward the same genetically predetermined destiny, the psychologists' observations might be taken as universal. But the assumptions that underlie this experiment are, in fact, hopelessly parochial. For example, to the street kids of Rio de Janeiro, where tens of thousands of children, some of them quite young, live virtually unsupervised, common sense might tell Miss Puppet to eat the chocolate right away before somebody else wolfs it down. And instead of wasting time deciding which drawer to look in, check both of them quickly and grab whatever goodies she can. Measured against the psychologists' comfortable middle class standards, the shrewdest street kids would probably be considered learning disabled.

I tried the hidden-chocolate experiment with my niece Hanna Lang-St. Marie, who had turned three years old two weeks earlier. In which drawer, I asked her, did she think the puppet would look for the chocolate? Hanna, who wants for nothing materially, shrugged and suggested that I ask the puppet myself. Seemed pretty darn sensible to me.

The CS Reality Check

Common sense shows itself in real-world situations and spontaneous problems rather than those calculated, however adroitly, to test and challenge the mind. I bought Hanna a clever little board game, Mr. Mighty Mind, in which children choose among six geometric shapes and fit them into design cards of increasing complexity; level one is matching the two halves of a circle. This game was recommended to me as exactly the kind of activity used to develop and test a preschooler's common sense. At this writing I don't know how Hanna has taken to Mr. Mighty Mind, though I'll bet she does fine. Yet some children, perhaps just as commonsensical, care nothing about matching two plastic halves of a toy circle, but would zing right into the problem, say, of fitting together two halves of a broken plate. Especially if they had broken it.

Whether the pieces of Tyrone's fractured self-concept can ever be fitted back together is impossible to say. Peculiar as it seems, if my guess that the boy was about four years old is correct, time may have run out. The current psychological consensus says that's the age when the common-sense die is cast: "Most investigators now agree that something important happens at about the age of 4 in the child's acquisition of the common-sense view of the world. At this age, they begin to form the concept of mind, rather than simply noting isolated mental phenomena," writes Forguson. Assessing the current psychological consensus, he says once a child understands that there is such a thing as a mind, and that he or she and everyone else has one, the components of common-sense understanding are set. Or as Robert Fulghum might say, All we really need to know we learn by kindergarten.

4

How Is Common Sense Taught?

The Berea Method

"Common sense? Believe me, this place has got nothing to do with common sense," says John P. Stephenson, president of Berea College, a small liberal-arts college nestled in the blue-grass foothills of eastern Kentucky.

Does formal education transform the basic common sense that we naturally develop into "good common sense," which the *Oxford English Dictionary* calls "general sagacity; combined fact and readiness in dealing with the everyday affairs of life"? If so, why does it seem that what we learn at school is frequently irrelevant and even downright obstructive to our acquiring the simple practical wisdom with which all healthy minds are endowed?

"See that portrait behind my desk? That man's eyes burn holes in my back every day." President Stephenson, a trim middle-aged gentleman, pivots in his spindle-backed chair to show me the imaginary holes in his crisp white shirt, then gestures helplessly toward the wall behind him. There the stern countenance of the founder, Reverend John G. Fee, shines not with good common sense but with the holy mania of a soul possessed by the "gospel of impartial love."

If ever there was a tilter at windmills, it was the Reverend Fee, who believed that God loved equally all He had seen fit to create, black and white, woman and man. This was as obvious to the Scotch-Irish minister from Ohio as that people exist at all. Thus, seven years before the Civil War, or the War of Northern Aggression as it was known thereabout, Fee, his wife, and their three small children set out for Kentucky, a slaveholding state where they had secured a ten-acre homestead. Encouraged by a small stipend from the American Missionary Association of New York City, the Fee family did Christ's work and founded Berea, a nonslaveholding interracial community named after the town in Acts of the Apostles (17:10), where "women of standing as well as men" received the holy word from the apostles Silas and Paul.

"Believing as we did that we were exactly where the Lord would have us, we lay down and slept calmly, sweetly," writes Fee in his autobiography. Soon enough, however, the good reverend set some of the neighbors to tossing and turning.

Just as Paul had his run-ins with the Thessalonians, quite a few Kentuckians took offense at Fee's conviction that "God hath made of one blood all nations of men," seeing as how such talk might encourage the slaves to bolt for the freedom that lay just across the Ohio River. Yet even the slaveholders had to admit that the Fees, and their friends, John A. R. Rogers and his wife, who also came via Ohio to help start up the community, were hard folks to hate, the way they invited everyone into their one-room slab school to learn how to read scripture, do ciphers, and generally get along in life. And unlike a lot of those northern abolitionist hotheads, the reverend did preach a gospel of nonviolence with a nonsectarian, come-one-come-all Christian theology that still suffuses Berea today.

Of course it helped to have a friend like Cassius Marcellus Clay, the man who gave the Fees their Kentucky start. He packed two pistols and a knife. Clay, in whose honor the great heavyweight boxing champion from Louisville, Muhammad Ali, was first named, was a shrewd, rich, power-hungry gambling man. To his way of thinking, moral meant smart and immoral meant stupid meant slavery, which he saw as Godawful bad business. The old common-sense assumption that the slaves' unwaged labor gave the South a vital economic edge was dead wrong. Just look around, he argued, and use your common sense. See how things have turned out: "Clay emphasized the evils arising from slavery: depression of education, manufactures, agriculture, the fine arts, and constitutional liberties, as well as the encouragement pressed upon white nonslaveholding people to emigrate from Kentucky because of the low condition of their economic life and their schools," write Elizabeth S. Peck and Emily Ann Smith in *Berea's First 125 Years*.

Clay reckoned that if Berea came out a success he would be glad to take the credit, preferably in gubernatorial form. But Fee, author of *An Antislavery Manual*, had taken to importing guest speakers from Oberlin College in Ohio, a school with a wide reputation for being "anti-slavery, anti-caste, anti-rum, anti-sin." Never a way to get up a good party, even a political one.

After a particularly absolutist July 4 speech in which Fee refused to compromise with the slaveholders in any way, Clay withdrew his political patronage, though still lip-servicing Berean ideals. As the war drew near, the mobs grew more agitated but Fee remained steadfastly nonviolent, even in self-defense. No one in the family ever took up a weapon. Well, Mrs.

Fee once took to filling a syringe with harsh vinegar and laying it aside of her bed to spray any intruders who might come in during the night. But she soon repented.

Two weeks after John Brown's abolitionist raid in Virginia, ninety-four Bereans were run out of Kentucky, mostly back across the river into Ohio. Though Kentucky eventually sided with the Union when war broke out, the Fees and the Rogers were not welcomed back into this ambivalent state, and so they spent much of the war ministering to the families of black soldiers in the Union Army. Unlike white soldiers, who were allowed to shelter their families in the army camp over the winter, black soldiers' loved ones had to go out and fend for themselves. Thankfully, the Bereans helped put a stop to that. By the time hostilities ended, Reverend Fee had also managed to raise about $10,000 for his embryonic college, a nifty bit of salesmanship considering that he wasn't officially allowed to set foot on the campus he promised to build. But by 1866, the year after the war ended, Berea College enrolled its first class of "96 Negroes and 91 whites." And from the very earliest days, Gentlemen and Ladies were graduated in roughly equal numbers.

"Health!! Brains!! Pluck!!" were basic requirements to get a Berea education, according to an end-of-the-century recruitment poster. But in 1904, a flaming bigot by the name of Carl Day persuaded the Kentucky state legislature to pass the perfidious Day Law, which made it "unlawful for any person, corporation or association of persons to maintain or operate any college, school or institution where persons of the white and Negro races are both received as pupils for instruction." The purpose, according to Day, was to avoid "contaminating" the white students.

After fighting the Day Law all the way to the U.S. Supreme Court, Berea College trustees rejected a plan to move north, and instead endowed the Lincoln Institute, a college in Louisville founded exclusively for black students. Not until 1950, when the Day Law was partially repealed, did blacks return to Berea. By that time Berea had shifted its focus to Appalachia, at first by sending teachers, speakers and traveling libraries into the mountains by mail train, riverboat and mule-back, and eventually by founding Berea's service program, which has been renovating and equipping rural schools, running adult-education programs, setting up dental clinics, and funding meal programs ever since. All courtesy of the faculty, staff and students.

Today, the Berea College Appalachian Center keeps the Great Smokies culture steaming with weaving, storytelling, poetry and music, culminating each Christmas with a folk-dancing festival that attracts experts and enthusiasts from all over the world. Current college guidelines state that 80 percent of the students must come from the surrounding mountain region, with 15 percent from nonmountain areas, and 5 percent from abroad. Because relatively few African-Americans now live in the Appalachians, their proportion of Berea's enrollment has dropped to about 10 percent, though the figure may be on the rise if one of Stephenson's pet projects, the "Black Mountain Improvement Association", which promotes black-youth potential in the Appalachian region, brings in a crop of new recruits.

Despite its travails—or because of them, depending on your theology—Berea has gone on to become a great American success story. It is the only private college in the country where *all* students attend tuition free, and where *all* students, including the children of alumni, faculty and staff, come from low-income households. For their entire four-year stay at Berea, all students work ten to twenty hours weekly in a labor program that provides pocket money and instills the work ethic as an integral part of their education.

What with all its requirements, commitments and restrictions, Berea might be excused if the academics weren't quite up to snuff. Yet even here, this "little college that could" is at the top of the class. Its graduates are second in the South and third in the nation in earning doctorates. In 1987 and 1988, *US News and World Report* ranked Berea as the number one institution among smaller, comprehensive colleges and universities in the United States. The newsmagazine recently moved the school into a larger competitive category, putting it up against universities with full graduate and professional programs. Berea, alas, has fallen to number three.

Since its quixotic beginnings as a missionary outpost in a strife-torn slaveholding state, the Berea method for teaching common sense has been to fly right in the face of it. "Lots of people seem to think that our system at Berea just makes good sense and that with $50 to $60 million you could build another one. But what it really takes to create a place like this is a radical cause that makes you swim against humanity for a hundred years," says Stephenson. Though developed by wild-eyed dreamers, the Berea method has solid practical lessons for all levels of education, from postgraduate study to the ABCs.

First, Everybody Works

What was your first job as a child? Feeding the dog? Helping set the table for dinner? Did you get paid a weekly allowance, so much per job, or was work around the house just something you had to do? If your pay bore any relation to the work performed, then you might have tried to come up with things to get paid for. Raking up the leaves was worth something. Raking up the flowers was not. Counting loudly up to a thousand by ones just to get fifty cents out of your mother was *definitely* not. Shoveling snow off the sidewalks in front of the church was a nice idea, but the kids who got to dig out the doctor's Cadillac made five bucks each!

Working teaches common sense. Though it may not be provable scientifically, good work habits and good judgment beget and reinforce each other much as physical fitness and mental alertness are steady partners in life. Youngsters who grow up working around the home, at school, and in the neighborhood just seem to accumulate more good common sense. And the more common sense they get, the better they will do at the jobs they go on to hold. If the primary goal of a nation's educational system is to produce an able labor force, doesn't common sense say that the system ought to teach its students the value of work?

Many American schools honor the value of labor in their curricula. Most, though, do not. Certainly not as in many other countries—notably Japan—where from the first day of school through the end of compulsory education in ninth grade, at age fifteen, students and teachers are responsible for keeping the classroom and grounds clean and otherwise helping out the janitorial support staff in maintaining their schools. The theory is that simple labor builds character and maturity. Students responsible for maintaining their physical surroundings are less likely to mess things up. And also less likely to screw things up when they go into the workaday world. Plus, it saves money.

Since the 1890s, the Berea Labor Program has sought to demonstrate "that work, manual and mental, has dignity as well as utility." Students are employed as groundskeepers, laboratory assistants, office clerks, teaching aides, waiters and waitresses at the on-campus Boone Tavern Hotel, in local hospitals, on Berea's nearby 1,200-acre farm, in its 7,700-acre forest, and even in the power and water utilities, which the college runs for the town. Wages averaging about $2 an hour can keep the kids in pocket money in a town where a dollar can buy lunch. The net result is that the students are responsible for physically maintaining their community.

"The labor program is just one more way for a student to feel good about herself or himself. It's another way to build up self-confidence, which is really important since a lot of the students here don't have that much when they start out. And if you do good work, you get a raise," says Krista Bender, whose job, when I visited, was to give the campus tour.

Could the Beverly Hills 90210 generation hack it at Berea? Would they deign to? One advantage that Berea students gain from their disadvantaged backgrounds is that they grow up with lots of jobs to do: "Most of the students at Berea are used to working at home, caring for family members, helping out with chores, things like that. For them, work is something they're used to, and something they expect to do. I'm not sure college students coming from more affluent families would have such an easy time getting used to that," says Sally Blakey Capobianco, class of 1959, whose mother, brother and sister also went to Berea.

Maybe today's youths are just plain spoiled. Not according to William Myers, a United Nations Children's Fund (UNICEF) educational specialist who believes that they are actually deprived of the opportunity to work. Myers is writing a book reexamining the benefits of elementary work in educational curricula. He believes that in Anglo-American culture the idea of youngsters doing physical labor in an institution hits a spot still sore from residual guilt and revulsion over child-labor abuses during nineteenth-century industrialization. Contending that we have gone too far the other way, "protecting" children from the very activity which, if properly monitored, will build their character and endurance, Myers argues that students deserve to be exposed to whatever builds their character best, including supervised physical labor.

Then again, why make a virtue out of dull toil? Manual labor isn't what people want to do, it's what they have to do if they can't find anything better, right? Why shouldn't our nation's precious posterity be protected from drudgery that dims the wits and dampens the spirits? With winning, insidious arguments like these, we can see little hope for school labor programs any time soon. On the theory that competition will improve educational quality just as it improves the commercial marketplace, most current plans for American educational reform encourage competition between schools, either with a voucher system for choosing between public and private schools or simply among public schools in a district. Which school do you think would win most students—a Berealike secondary school where students are required to empty wastepaper baskets, pick up litter from the schoolyard, and so on, bearing Berea's motto, *Vincit Qui Patitur,* "He who suffers conquers"; or a franchised version of Beverly Hills High?

President Clinton declared that a national-service program for teenagers and young adults was one of his long-term domestic policy goals. Maybe school labor programs, similar to the ones already in operation in many other school systems around the world, would be a good first step, simpler and far less costly than starting up a full national-service campaign. All he'd have to do to get it started is ask that schools require their students to help clean up. Much as President Kennedy dramatically made physical fitness an American educational goal, Clinton could do the same for school labor. Working could become as trendy as working out, or as politically correct as recycling.

Common Sense Is Rewarded

Like anything else, common sense is promoted by being rewarded and inhibited by being punished or ignored. By this measure, is common sense being taught in our educational system today?

Maybe things have changed for the CS better since I was in the second grade at the South Street public school in Danbury, Connecticut. In my class was a girl named Margaret, who was repeating the grade. Margaret was the teacher's pet, Mrs. Keane's super-pupil who could do any job: run down to the principal's office, collect the homework papers, run the Victrola, and generally manage anything extra or special that needed to be done. One week, Margaret was out sick and Mrs. Keane chose me to be her helper. When it came to book smarts, I was at the top of the class, but after a day or two of Margaret's job. . . . I don't remember all the details from thirty-odd years ago but I do recall lots of knocking into things and being generally confused. One rainy day, as recess time approached, the teacher asked me to go down the hall to the schoolyard door and see how hard it was raining. Robotically, I went to the wardrobe, dragged out my yellow slicker and galoshes and began pulling it all on. After a minute or two, Mrs. Keane caught sight of what was going on, exclaimed something unpleasant, and sent someone else down to just stick their head out the door. Common sense!

Mrs. Keane appreciated Margaret, especially her first day back, but over the long haul most school systems reward and advance booksmarts over Margaret's can-do competence. Common sense is a widely esteemed mental attribute, yet almost nowhere in our educational system is it explicitly taught, learned or even acknowledged. It is deeply undervalued in the general scholastic scheme. You get no grade in it, except sometimes in those secondary report-card marks for work habits and effort. To my knowledge, no awards are given for "Most Common Sense." Perhaps it is time to establish, like the National Honor Society, the National Common Sense Society, to honor the Margarets among our students.

Instead of being honored, the Margarets tend to be ignored, particularly if they are minority students, according to educational sociologist Jeannie Oakes. In *Keeping Track: How Schools Structure Inequality* (Yale University Press), Oakes methodically demonstrates the poverty of educational tracks for manual and service training: "Very few teachers . . . used vocational topics as an avenue to general education in any broader sense: the acquisition of academic skills, personal development or social understanding." Anticipating the current political vogue for expanding the nation's vocational–technical training and apprenticeship programs, Oakes argues that this approach will just result in more black and other minority students being shunted into educational obscurity. "Expanded vocational emphasis is likely to continue to sort students along racial and economic lines. In view of our findings, school people and policy makers should seriously reconsider the appropriateness of vocational training in secondary schools." Perhaps Oakes's conclusions are a bit ivory-tower considering the pressing necessity to provide employment for minority teenagers, yet her point about segregation—of black from white, manual from mental, laborer from academic—is certainly well taken at Berea, where integration of races, sexes and skills is the method that works.

Ironically, the same kind of training that in so many schools substitutes for education is used, at Berea, to broaden students' horizons. The jewel of the college's labor curriculum is its crafts program, a vertically integrated enterprise that employs 10 to 15 percent of the current 1,500-student enrollment. In the woodcrafts sector, maple, oak and other hardwoods are grown in the college's forest and shipped to the campus facilities, where students make craft items that are then packaged and mailed to fill orders generated by a sophisticated direct-marketing program reaching customers around the United States and overseas. Berea crafts have become so popular that the school is unable to meet its Japanese demand. How many MBA programs, or for that matter, corporations run by MBA degree-holders, can boast a trade surplus with Japan?

Berea could easily meet the demand for its crafts and increase its profits by hiring skilled graduates; most of the expense in making fine woodcrafts, ceramics, woven goods, and metalworks comes in teaching beginners how to master their craft. Doesn't common sense suggest hanging on to the best workers once they've acquired these valuable skills? "Just when they get good, they have to leave," complains Garry Barker, director of marketing for Berea College Crafts. Barker explains that the crafts program has a specific rule against hiring anyone ever enrolled at the college because it might be tempting for students, particularly those from the poorest families, to drop out and take jobs. Thus the crafts program, like the overall labor program, breaks even, at best. It is not for the revenue that Berea remains so tenaciously dedicated to the proposition that all students should work with their hands and their back, as well as their head.

There's an old saying to the effect that if you want to get a job done, give it to someone who's busy. At Berea, everybody seems busy, always headed somewhere, with not much in the way of just hanging around. Along with studies, jobs, and service programs, each student is required to attend at least ten assembly programs per semester, and to meet various other participation requirements. "You can get thrown out of here more ways than just flunking," grumbles Ms. Bender. Seems to take some common sense just to keep track of everything that's got to be done.

Making It All Add Up

Of all the basic subjects, mathematics can seem the most alien to common sense. It is heavily self-referential, relying more on internal consistency than on correspondence with general human experience. And the more self-referential a discipline, the less accessible it is to common-sense reasoning, explains Lionel Elvin in *The Place of Commonsense in Educational Thought* (1977). So alien is math to some students' sensibilities that recently a movement has been started to reclassify mathematical competence as more of a talent or special ability than as a basic intellectual component. Traditionalists count their fingers and retort that the language of numbers is every bit as natural as the language of words.

In math, as in any other language, it all depends on how you put it. Ask Margaret, Quick, what's twenty-four times three? and the second-grader may freeze. But if you asked her instead to make sure that everyone in the class got three sheets of construction paper, she'd count up the students (if she didn't know that number by heart already) take out a good-sized stack of paper from the supply closet, and come pretty close pretty quick. Smarter than a more literal-minded, "better" student might be in calculating that seventy-two sheets were needed, counting them off the pile, and then distributing them.

The ability to make quick, general quantity judgments is valuable in life and, as we saw in Chapter 1 with Dr. Karen Wynn's studies of five-month-old infants, quite possibly an innate human trait. Yet rarely is it rewarded in school.

"Estimation is generally not taught either, aside from a few lessons on rounding off numbers. The connection is rarely made that rounding off and making reasonable estimates have something to do with real life. Grade-school students aren't invited to estimate the number of bricks in the side of a school wall, or how fast the class speedster runs, or the percentage of students with bald fathers, or the ratio of one's head's circumference to one's height, or how many nickels are necessary to make a tower equal in height to the Empire State building, or whether all those nickels would fit in their classroom," writes John Allen Paulos. The Temple University mathematics professor argues forcefully that the general ability to handle numbers, judge amounts, and estimate unknowns is in many ways as important as the ability to read.

Lacking the proper mathematical training, most people use common sense, or what passes for it, to estimate quantity and probability. According to psychologist Chris Dracup of Newcastle Polytechnic, in England, writing in *Royal Statistical Society News* (May 1991), we rely on three rules of thumb. The first, known as availability, judges frequency and probability by how easily examples of the events can be brought to mind. The second, called representatives, holds that the untrained observer assesses the probability that a person or event belongs to a group depending on the extent to which he, she, or it has the significant characteristics of the class; the "if it looks like a duck, smells like a duck . . ." argument. Finally, the anchoring-and-adjustment rule of thumb is that most of us are insecure in making estimates, and that we therefore tend to agree with any initial estimates that are available. In short, most people are so uncomfortable with numbers that they look at any nonquantitative guidelines they can to get them through the exercise.

Question: If Mary can swim one mile in half an hour, how far can she swim in an hour and a half? Three hours? One day? A year?

Common sense says people get tired. Unless Mary is a super-human android, simple multiplication will not yield the right answers. Yet from elementary school on, we are programmed by problems like these to divorce math from reality, to pick out the numbers and perform functions upon them. We become so caught up in getting the "right answer"—three miles in an hour and a half, six miles in three hours, and so on—that we miss the obvious point.

In my experience, about the best way to get comfortable with numbers is to put a dollar sign in front of them. Some of us just like a little extra incentive to get thinking. When I was about five, my grandfather, Habib Haddad, would dig deep into his pocket for a handful of change and then bounce the coins one by one across the living room rug. I would scamper after them and if, by the time I had caught up with the last one, I had also correctly added up the total in my hand, I could keep the money. If not, all the loot went back to grandpa. Not only did my grandfather's common-sense approach make me quick at addition, it also taught me a valuable lesson—that what's worth least in life can give you most trouble—in this case, pennies.

If you are really good at numbers, odds are you can eventually get your hands on some money, either by managing it, accounting it, investing it, or gambling it. I am reminded of this point whenever I visit the Korean fruit and vegetable markets throughout New York City. There men and women who can barely speak English, much less read it, know their business math cold. And Paulos points out that innumeracy is also a women's issue: "I've seen too many bright women go into sociology and too many dull men go into business, the only difference between them being that the men managed to scrape through a couple of college math courses."

Berea students get the course work, the opportunity for business experience, and one other lesson in just how critical numbers can be. Perhaps you've wondered how the college makes ends meet, with no tuition, no government aid, and no profit from the labor program. The Reverend Fee's silver tongue for fundraising quivers in the mouths of all good Bereans. Kentucky is a poor state but with a lot of sinful profit in it, mainly from bourbon, horses, and tobacco: high margin, high guilt, high donor yield. And Kentuckians, wherever they go, are likely to form Kentuckian societies, where every year around Derby time the Berea gospel gets sung and the hat gets passed to the lucky winners. Then there's the ever-widening web of supporters like the late Alex Haley who, though not an alumnus or otherwise connected to the college, become trustees, fundraisers and general apostles of the Berea way. Just by reading this chapter, the likelihood has increased that the Bereans will find you and extract a sizable donation.

Berea College manages to raise an average of more than $3 million a year in donations, and has amassed an endowment in excess of $200 million. These people really do know their numbers. In 1987, *The New York Times* reported that Berea's investments fared better than those of Harvard, Yale and Princeton. A good thing too, Stephenson reminds me, "because an awful lot of alumni get really angry because they're too rich for their kids to go here." Still, more than three-fifths of Berea graduates contribute to their alma mater, one of the highest participation rates in the country.

Where does Berea find such exemplary characters, who work well, study well, and then give selflessly for the rest of their born days? As mentioned, four-fifths of the student body is drawn from the surrounding mountain region, but how does selection work among them? Amid the desperate, inbred poverty of Appalachia, many Berea students come from families that might be classified as dysfunctional and have problems that might be classified as learning disabilities. If, that is, anyone ever got around to classifying them. Doesn't it seem that the more psychologists per unit of population, the more disability labels will be affixed? And that once those labels go on they stay on, like an indelible psychological tattoo? "The amazing thing about the students here is that just about everyone seems to have gone through something incredible. It seems like everybody's got a story that would just ruin them for the rest of their lives—but, you know, it doesn't," explains Ms. Bender.

Berea's admissions procedure relies heavily on recommendations by teachers, guidance counselors and others who know and have worked with the applicants. Academic performance is a big factor, yet all that Berea can really boast is that most of its applicants rank in the top two-fifths of their high-school class. Least important, when considered at all, are the results of standardized tests.

Yacht is to regatta as roach is to . . .

That line is a mocking example of cultural bias in standardized intelligence tests. A child raised in an underprivileged community or a landlocked region such as the Kentucky hills might not know what a regatta is, yet could nonetheless be every bit as sensible as an upper-class child whose family owned the yacht club. Conversely, a wealthy child might also get the question wrong and be unfairly judged, or even a poor child who grows up in an area with no roaches but perhaps plenty of fleas.

Consider the subtler bias in this question, which did make it into some primary-school IQ tests:

Hat is to head as cup is to . . .
Answer: (a) table (b) saucer (c) face (d) chair.

The correct answer, (b) saucer, comes a lot more easily if one grows up in a home where such amenities are observed. The response, (a) table, would be just as sensible to a child raised in a less formal, less affluent home, such as the households where most Berea students were raised, in which cups and mugs are placed on the table as hats are placed on the head.

Psychologists Richard K. Wagner, at Florida State University, and Robert J. Sternberg, of Yale, charge that IQ tests, at most, measure *academic intelligence,* which is only a small subset of general intelligence. Building on the work of educational psychologist Ulrich Neisser, Wagner and Sternberg contend that tasks requiring academic intelligence tend to be artificially constructed in that they (1) are formulated by other people, (2) have little or no intrinsic interest, (3) have all the needed information available from the outset, (4) are external to an individual's ordinary experience, (5) usually are well defined, (6) have only one correct answer, and (7) usually have only one correct method of solution. In "Tacit Knowledge and Intelligence in the Everyday World," *practical intelligence* is defined as "responding appropriately in terms of one's long-range and short-range goals, given the actual facts of the situation as one discovers them." In short, intelligence tests miss some of the most useful kinds of smarts.

In his widely regarded *Frames of Mind: The Theory of Multiple Intelligences* (1983), Howard Gardner argues for a whole new mode of intelligence testing. He contends that educators overvalue such academic skills as logical, linguistic, and mathematical abilities and diminish or ignore others, such as the general hand–eye skills required in physical labor. With his theory of multiple intelligences, or M.I. theory, Gardner argues that rather than thinking of intelligence as an overall characteristic, stronger in some areas, weaker in others, the mind should be regarded as a collection of six relatively independent intelligences: linguistic, logical-mathematical, musical, spatial, bodily-kinesthetic, personal (a catch-all category for knowledge of self, social skills, and so on).

To no one's surprise, Gardner finds the techniques of standardized testing to be woefully inadequate: "Nearly all current [intelligence] tests are so devised that they call principally upon linguistic and logical facility (as well as a certain speed, flexibility and perhaps a certain superficiality as well). . . . Tests of the various intelligences must each be posed by appropriate means. Thus, a measure for bodily intelligence should involve the use of the body in such activities as learning a game or a dance (and not a set of questions about such activity); an assessment of spatial ability should involve navigation about an unfamiliar environment (and not a series of geometric rotations requiring multiple choice responses)," he writes.

True enough. It's one thing to answer questions about how to do the lambada and quite another to move across the floor. Likewise, a written driving exam bears little relation to the actual operation of a car, which is why both types of test are given. Disappointingly, Gardner suggests no way of measuring common sense, which he defines as "the ability to deal with problems in an intuitive, rapid, and perhaps unexpectedly accurate manner." (Isn't an "intuitive manner" both "rapid" and "perhaps unexpectedly accurate"?) Gardner buries common sense in a page at the back of his book, complaining that "far from being common coin, it seems to be applied preferentially to individuals with highly developed skills in one or two areas of intelligence [interpersonal and mechanical, by his reckoning] and not in the kind of 'across-the-board' manner implied by the term."

After years of wrangling over what to do about IQ tests, in 1986 the California Board of Regents decided to prohibit IQ tests in the state's public-school system—for black students only! What mixture of racist condescension and cosseting rationale led to this nonsensical decision, only masochists will venture to imagine. Common sense says that when judging a student's potential, go with the indicator that is most positive, because what a child has attained at any developmental stage is less important than what he or she can become. Some shy pupils are actually "discovered" by tests. Instead of giving African-American children this extra opportunity to shine, the Regents' approach, however much paved with good intentions, has been to deny and stigmatize them all. Recently, in response to a suit by a group of African-American parents, the ban was partially repealed, allowing black students to be IQ-tested, for "learning disabilities."

Jaime Escalante, the Los Angeles inner-city math teacher made famous in the film, *Stand and Deliver,* would prefer to see intelligence tests dropped altogether, arguing that they unfairly shunt students from non–English-speaking backgrounds into lower academic tracks. Escalante has made it a policy to admit any student willing to attempt his legendarily tough advanced-placement calculus course, and delights in reporting that the lower-track students have consistently outperformed those designated IQ gifted.

Escalante, who came from a technical career in the private sector, would be likely to agree with the conclusions of Wagner and Sternberg in "Tacit Knowledge in Managerial Success," a follow-up to their aforementioned study of intelligence testing: "An ability that counted more than IQ for managerial success, according to our informants, was common sense, or practical intelligence." Upon interviewing a variety of successful managers and executives, the psychologists found that real-world performance depends heavily on *tacit knowledge*, "knowledge that usually is not openly expressed or stated (*Oxford English Dictionary*, 1933)." Examples of tacit intelligence in the workplace include knowing how to overcome procrastination, reward good work or performance, and get your point across in conversation. A number of executives also agreed "that IQ and scores from other ability and achievement tests were not predictive of managerial success." Some even felt that a high IQ could deter success, because very intelligent workers might lose patience with and neglect important advice from others less intellectually capable. Too smart for their own good, was Wagner and Sternberg's basic finding.

Ironically, charges of bias and inadequacy have caused the testing industry to boom. Where traditionally they offered a handful of basics, such as Wechsler Adult Intelligence Scale (WAIS), Stanford-Binet, and Iowa Basic Skills, now we see a welter of new and exotic exams, particularly in special education, which seems to discover a new learning disability each month, and three new ways to test for it. Today the psychologists stock well over a hundred psychometric, diagnostic, aptitudinal and attitudinal measures, including a host of newfangled "word-attack" tests, picture-story–language tests, and other diagnostics aimed at the general and special-needs student body. Testing is out of control: the anxious desire to know how students are doing is overwhelming their real need, which is to progress and move on. "Teachers are confronted with the results of tests, checklists, scales and batteries on an almost daily basis," write John Salvia and James E. Ysseldyke in the introduction to the third edition of their *Assessment in Special and Remedial Education,* considered the bible of educational testing at the primary- and secondary-school levels.

"We don't care as much about what a student comes in with as what he leaves with," declared former Berea president Willis Weatherford, summarizing the school's educational philosophy. When it comes to standardized testing, good scores mean more than bad scores, and neither means a heck of a lot. Edward Ford, public-relations director for the college, observes, "Like any other college we look at the applicant's test scores, SATs, IQ and the others. But if a counselor says that an applicant really has the potential to become a good college student, even if the applicant has low test scores, we'll generally weigh the personal opinion more heavily than the numbers."

A sound CS attitude—adapting an old British saying about morality—is better caught than taught. The best way to teach common sense is to act sensibly, which is also the best way to attract sound-minded students to begin with. Berea College enhanced its own common-sense reputation in developing the Berea Community School. Conceived in the 1950s and born in 1965, the school for grades pre-K through 12 is the result of an unprecedented collaboration among a city government, a private college, and the public schools. First securing participation by the community with the passage of a school bond issue and school tax, and capital commitments from the city council, the College endowed the school with forty-five acres and a large cash donation, and then retired a portion of the bonds. Not far from Berea's original one-room schoolhouse now stands a public educational complex where an elementary school and a high school share gymnasium, indoor swimming pool, tennis courts, athletic fields, golf course, library, museums, science laboratories, observatory, greenhouse, environmental research center, computer center, crafts and industrial shops, television studio, theater, hiking trails, and more. More than 90 percent of the teachers have advanced degrees, and all participate in a continuing training program. No school labor, but unlike the vocational segregation that Oakes finds pervasive, the vo-tech program curriculum is well integrated into the overall academic scheme.

Educated Inability

Berowne. . . . What is the end of study? let me know.
King. Why, that to know, which else we should not know.
Berowne. Things hid and barr'd, you mean, from common sense?
King. Ay, that is study's god like recompense.

William Shakespeare, *Love's Labour's Lost,* I.I

Shakespeare reminds us that the purpose of higher education is to transcend the rudimentary, frequently shallow assumptions of status quo. But can too much education cloud the thinking? Or is this self-indulgent quibbling in face of the truth that education is one of the great blessings of life, uplifting all forms of knowledge and intelligence, including common sense? "I think the commmonsense view would be that from the exploratory movements of a baby onwards we do have drives that make us want to understand and that our success or otherwise depends largely on our general powers of mind; but that in an educated man these are shaped, improved and occasionally distorted by the disciplines he follows," writes Elvin.

Archibald MacLeish, the renowned poet and former Librarian of Congress, described education-induced distortion as "that peculiar disease of intellectuals, that infatuation with ideas at the expense of experience that compels experience to conform to bookish preconceptions." Although the idea probably dates back to the first absent-minded professor, "trained incapacity" was first formally advanced by the Norwegian-American economist Thorstein Veblen. Best known for coining the phrase "conspicuous consumption" in his major work, *The Theory of the Leisure Class* (1899), Veblen referred particularly to the "trained incapacity" of overeducated engineers and sociologists unable to understand issues that they would have been able to grasp if they had not had this training. Building on Veblen, Herman Kahn, the pioneering futurist who thought "the unthinkable" about the consequences of nuclear war, attacked "educated incapacity," which he defined as "an acquired or learned inability to understand or even perceive a problem, much less a solution," in *World Economic Development: 1979 and Beyond.* "When a possibility comes up that is ruled out by the accepted framework, an expert—or well-educated individual—is often less likely to see it than an amateur without the confining framework," he writes. Kahn uses the example of health care, where medical professionals, particularly physicians, have often been the last to accept unorthodox new treatments, such as antiseptic procedures for childbirth, vaccination against smallpox, and penicillin.

Kahn delighted in attacking the intellectual idiocy of individuals educated in the departments of psychology, sociology, history and the humanities, generally at leading United States universities. (He would have had fun at the expense of University of Washington psychologists, who after two years of research on suicide in the Seattle area concluded that the reason for the city's abnormally high rate was *not* its rainy, gloomy weather, although they couldn't say what it was.) The founder of the archconservative Hudson Institute usually targeted what he perceived as the liberal elite: "This is not to say that other groups might not be equally biased and illusioned—only that their illusions are generally reflected in more traditional ways," wrote Kahn.

Intellectuals of all stripes are vulnerable to educated incapacity, and some don't regret it a bit. If you can create a whole world within your mind, pleasing to your tastes and pliant to your whims, why pay any more attention than necessary to that messy, uncontrollable world around you? Gardner defines his most vital term: "An intelligence is the ability to solve problems, or to create products, that are valued within one or more cultural settings." By his definition, a drunken billionaire handing out bagfuls of hundred-dollar bills is an example of an intelligence, for that product would be valued in just about every known cultural setting. Why stretch a word out of shape? The natural human tendency is to pay compliments in terms of one's own attributes, and Gardner clearly is intelligent. But classifying all valuable abilities as intelligences is intellectual condescension, or at least wishful fuzzy-mindedness. Gardner falsely equates "abilities" with "intelligences," destroying the integrity and specificity of the latter term.

Educated inability becomes hazardous to the rest of us when that loss of common sense translates into public policy. Elvin gives the example of an educational psychologist at an international conference asserting, "there was no research evidence to support the idea that children learn better in small classes than in large ones." Now anyone who has ever sat in any classroom knows that the number of students is important, but statistics clouded that psychologist's natural judgment. It *is* true that in lecture classes there is not much difference between two hundred students and four hundred, assuming that the hall has room for everyone. But it is *not* true that no difference can be found in a seminar, or a grade-school class, between twenty students and forty. By lumping these qualitatively different situations, the numerical results may indeed seem inconclusive.

One would think the other educators would see right through this fallacy but Elvin writes, "And this has been resoundingly said time and time again until now influential fund-granting institutions like the World Bank seem uncritically to accept it." In the same vein, Elvin tells an even scarier story with this end: "As a result Professor Halpin, then of Chicago, had to get together a book of essays whose purpose, in part, was to explain to superintendents of schools that schools and factories were different. Those of us who had not been victims of such theorising might have been trusted to take this for granted."

It's sad and a little frightening when overeducation debilitates elemental, nonspecialized judgment. B. F. Skinner, the founding father of behavioral psychology, believed that human beings are flawed machines that can be improved by science. "The disastrous results of common sense in the management of behavior are evident in every walk of life, from international affairs to the care of a baby," he wrote in *About Behaviorism* (1974). Skinner argued, "we shall continue to be inept in these fields, until a scientific analysis clarifies the advantages of a more effective technology. It will then be obvious that the results are due to more than common sense." Skinner's own efforts to create a "more effective technology" included the "Skinner baby box"—a large, air-conditioned, ostensibly germ-free enclosure with levers geared to provide rewards to appropriate actions—in which he attempted to raise his own daughter "scientifically." Her subsequent years of psychological turmoil have proved instructive.

Unlearning Helplessness

The flip side of educated inability is the phenomenon of "learned helplessness", which psychologist Israel Colon defines as "belief in an inevitable destiny outside one's control." Rather than arising from too much formal education, learned helplessness is the crippling of judgment that results when too much time has been spent in the school of hard knocks. Associated with environments of uncontrollable and unpredictable stress, learned helplessness occurs most frequently in underprivileged and oppressed groups. In the example in Colon's study, inner-city blacks and Latinos refuse to wear their seat belts while driving, not for lack of knowing the dangers but in the debilitating belief that "you can't change your fate."

In Paint Lick, Kentucky, Jane B. Stephenson, the Berea president's wife, runs the New Opportunity School for Women, a tuition-free, three-week program that has helped more than one hundred middle-aged women make the transition from home life to the job market. Most of these women married in their teens and had children before completing high school; they had "learned" that their life was in the home. But their need to take control of their destiny and join the labor force is especially critical because "Jobs in the region's predominantly he-man economy of mining and logging have been giving way to automation and to diminishing supplies of coal and wood, leaving a growing number of unemployed and broken-spirited men," writes Peter T. Kilborn in *The New York Times,* which ran a front-page story on the Berea College program.

I submit that most or all of these women would (1) agree that not every valuable ability, like having a baby at fourteen, is intelligent, and (2) say that of course it matters how many students a teacher has to look after in a class. More to the point

of educated inability, the professors, social workers, psychologists and other trained professionals from Berea College who
work with these women would, I submit, see things in pretty
much the same way. A good thing about common sense is that
it tends to be catching. The best way to cure educated inability
is to make sure that those with all the education keep in touch
with common folks.

Berea springs from faith in the cause of Christ, yet as much as
any other college, secular or religious, it ministers to practical
human needs. How sad that our federal government has been
caught in the opposite paradox, created, as it was, in the revolutionary cause of common-sense philosophy.

5

What Is the Common-Sense Philosophy?

Samuel Johnson's Toe

One sunny summer day on the southern coast of England, Samuel Johnson marched up to a boulder and with a mighty blow smacked his toe square against it. By most lights a stupid thing to do. Yet ever since that pivotal afternoon in 1763 an august procession of scholars, philosophers, and literati have paid homage to this self-inflicted injury as the consummate act of enlightenment, the ultimate argument for the Age of Reason, and the crowning achievement of the Great Cham, as he is known to devotees, the common-sense philosopher king.

Johnson was vexed with his rival, Bishop George Berkeley, an idealist who contended that all objects are really "collections of ideas" that do not "materially exist" outside the mind. And because whatever exists inside the mind is, by definition, an idea, it was just common sense that stones are ideas as well. This really got Johnson's goat. As I mentioned, common-sense philosophy assumes the existence of an objective physical world which we all share and which exists whether we perceive it or not. Johnson had had it with Berkeley, Descartes, David Hume, and all the other skeptics who spent years on end doubting their senses and writing about how ideas, particularly their own, were more real than the physical reality that everyone else plainly perceived. Fed up with philosophers who liked to "perplex the confines of distinction to buttress a point by mystification," the Great Cham delivered his swift kick in the rebuttal to remind them all just how much substance the kingdom of this world actually has.

So who's got more common sense, (1) the one who argues that stones are just ideas, or (2) the one who thwacks his toe trying to prove otherwise? Johnson knew full well that he didn't disprove any theories by kicking a rock. The skeptics didn't claim that objects were without substance or that a foot would pass right through them, and they would glibly respond that his aching toe was just another (bad) idea.

Johnson's frustrated response was less of a counterargument than a stubborn refusal to dignify a debate that he felt was pointless: "Practical wisdom is enlightenment by instinct, and part of its instinct is a kick at those who inspect too closely. Put another way, common sense is the 'sun' of the mind that renders itself both difficult and painful to see . . . it would have been dangerous to ask Johnson further, at the moment of his mighty kick, about the premises of his attack on Berkeley," writes Alan Liu in "Toward a Theory of Common Sense: Beckford's *Vathek* and Johnson's *Rasselas*."

As a scholar of the first order, Johnson validates our own lay suspicions that even if we can't quite follow it all, some very high-level BS is going on within the intellectual elite. Best known as the creator and editor-in-chief of *A Dictionary of the English Language* (1755), which is generally considered the language's first comprehensive reference work, he wrote, "The next best thing to knowing something is knowing where to find it."

And the place to find sense, which he defined as "Understanding; soundness of faculties; strength of natural reason," was in Alexander Pope's "Epistle to Burlington", which Johnson quoted to illustrate the definition:

> Something there is more needful than Expence,
> And something previous ev'n to Taste—'tis Sense:
> Good Sense, which only is the Gift of Heav'n,
> And tho' no science, fairly worth the sev'n:
> A Light, which in yourself you must perceive.

Dictionary Johnson's toe was a casualty in a general common-sense upheaval rumbling through much of the Western world. It started in France as a revolt against the philosophical elitism of René Descartes, who had quipped, "Common sense is the most equitably shared thing in the world, for every man is convinced that he is well supplied with it." This egalitarian movement became politicized during the chaos following the death of the Sun King, Louis XIV, and caught fire in 1720, when Louis XV staked virtually the entire national economy, currency and all, on a very shady Scotsman's preposterous scheme to plunder Mississippi, a place he had never even visited and to which he had no legal claim! Jesuit Claude Buffier was the first to formulate the common-sense philosophy, inveighing against skepticism and solipsism, the proposition that the self is the only thing that can be known and therefore that the self is the only thing that certainly exists. After Buffier came Jean Meslier, another French Jesuit who in 1762, after thirty years in the monastery and in the name of common sense, denounced all religion as irretrievably absurd.

The most influential school of common-sense philosophy arose from a group of thinkers known as the Wise Club, in Aberdeen, Scotland. Their leader was Thomas Reid, who formulated his doctrine of primary truths and first principles in *An Inquiry into the Human Mind on the Principles of Common Sense* (1764). Invoking the practical wisdom of the common man, Reid declared that in matters of common sense, "the learned and the unlearned, the philosopher and the day-labourer, are upon a level." An intellectual is no more likely to have common sense than the shopkeeper on the corner. Like Johnson, Reid bridled at the philosophical doctrine that because human senses are faulty, we can be certain only of our own thoughts: "Reason, says the skeptic, is the only judge of truth, and you ought to throw off every belief that is not grounded on reason[ing]. Why, sir, should I believe the faculty of reason more than that of perception?—they came both out of the same shop, and were made by the same artist; and if he puts one piece of false ware into my hands, what should hinder him from putting another?"

James Beattie, another Wise guy, summarized their creed: "Common sense hath, in modern times, been used by philosophers, both French and English, to signify that belief, not by progressive argumentation, but by an instantaneous, instinctive and irresistible impulse; derived neither from education nor from habit, but from nature." Gut feeling over logical argument; the great egalitarian spirit of common-sense philosophy is that everyone has their own personal take on the subject, and there's no telling by culture, historical period, professional discipline, or anything else whose opinions will be legitimate.

As we shall see, the problem with this common-sense philosophy of primary truths and first principles is that no one could ever quite agree on what those utterly obvious truths and principles were, exactly. As evidenced, for example, by the redoubtable Johnson's commonsensical analysis of the American Revolution: "Sir, they are a parcel of convicts, and ought to be thankful for any thing we allow them short of hanging. . . . I am willing to love all mankind, except an American," he exclaimed. According to biographer James Boswell, Johnson was seized with "inflammable corruption bursting into horrid fire, he breathed out threatenings and slaughter; calling them, 'Rascals—Robbers—Pirates'; and exclaiming, he'd 'burn and destroy them' " (*Life*).

The Common-Sense Revolution

Odd as it seems today, common sense was fast becoming a radical concept, an antiauthoritarian declaration of faith in the collective wisdom of the common folk and a rebellion against elitist intellectualism. Back in the days when the democratic form of government was considered about as risky, say, as self-rule for prison inmates would seem today, common-sense egalitarianism was insurrectionary indeed. Scottish pragmatism was just a skipstone away from Yankee ingenuity, and the common-sense philosophy soon found a home in revolutionary America. Not for nothing was Thomas Paine's founding polemic named *Common Sense*.

"O! ye that love mankind! Ye that dare oppose not only the tyranny but the tyrant, stand forth! Every spot of the Old World is overrun with oppression. Freedom hath been hunted round the globe. Asia and Africa have long expelled her. Europe regards her as a stranger and England hath given her warning to depart. O! receive the fugitive and prepare in time an asylum for mankind." To Thomas Paine, it was only common sense that America go to war against England and wage a long and bloody battle, outmanned and undergunned, against the mother country to whom we were bound by blood, language, and culture.

Paine's mission was to sell the idea of immediate armed struggle to an American public who, by most historical accounts, were about one-third in favor, one-third neutral and one-third opposed. A tough job, but throughout history leaders have usually found a way to overcome the masses' common-sense arguments for staying alive. (Paine did have the advantage that, as an Englishman who had emigrated to the United States only in 1774, he was unfettered by undue emotional attachments to the people whose lives and homeland would be wrecked by the war he espoused.) His genius lay in his ability to portray radical action as the only reasonable course:

"It is repugnant to reason, to the universal order of things, to all examples from former ages, to suppose that this continent can longer remain subject to any external power . . ." declared Paine, appealing to everyman's grasp of the obvious. The gulf between us was as wide and deep as the Atlantic Ocean, went his common-sense argument for American secession. Armed struggle was the inescapable price of freedom, logic could not help but conclude. (How unreasonable those Canadians and Australians have since proven to be, gaining their independence from that same external oppressor without firing a shot.)

Paine's patron, Philadelphia physician Benjamin Rush, brought the fiery manuscript to the attention of Benjamin Franklin, America's most popular common-sense philosopher. Despite Franklin's deep ambivalence toward war with Britain— right up to the eve of the revolution he preached that "There never was a good war or a bad peace"—our founding pundit had a weakness for a well-turned phrase, in this case, Paine's. Thus the legendary publisher of *Poor Richard's Almanack* gave *Common Sense* an edit, and the blessing it needed to be published widely. The pamphlet became an immediate national bestseller, sparking hot debates about democracy, independence, and the means necessary to wrest control from King George III, "the royal brute of Britain." Although John Adams, a stout patriot who would become the second United States president, denounced the pamphlet as either "honest ignorance or knavish hypocrisy," Paine bragged that *Common Sense* was popular "beyond anything since the invention of printing."

If one were to date the American Revolution from its intellectual commencement, the year would be 1690, the place would be England, and the hero, John Locke. Both Paine's *Common Sense* and the *Declaration of Independence,* written mostly by Thomas Jefferson, were heavily derived from Locke's *Two Treatises on Civil Government.* The towering English philosopher of freedom held that people are naturally happy, reasonable and tolerant, and that a government is bound by social contract to guarantee them the fundamental rights of "life, health, liberty and possessions" that they deserve. Hence Jefferson's "We hold these truths to be self-evident, that all men are created equal, that they are endowed by their Creator with certain unalienable Rights, that among these are Life, Liberty, and the pursuit of Happiness." Common-sense philosophy had produced fantastic intellectual synergy between thinkers on both sides of the Atlantic, but never true consensus. Somehow it seems sensible, in an illogical sort of way, that the most everyone could agree on was revolution, which Locke advocated as "a device for bringing happiness" to people whose governments had failed to live up to their end of the deal.

When it came to the actual blood-and-guts battle, common sense told Paine that the best way to gain happiness through revolution was to talk other people into doing the real work. He spent the wartime ensconced writing the sixteen-part chronicle, *The American Crisis.* Franklin, who upon signing the Declaration had warned that "We must all hang together, or assuredly we will hang separately," managed to hang loose in Paris as an American agent, following his own advice, "Keep your eyes wide open before marriage, half shut afterwards," with the revolution he had wed.

Jefferson stayed in the thick of things, spending the last years of the war as governor of Virginia. One might have thought that after the long and bitter war, he might welcome a little lighthearted escapism. Instead, Jefferson propounded the hardheaded belief that fiction is a preposterous way to diffuse truth. "Novels are an insidious obstacle to good education because they destroy our natural respect for reason and fact, plain and unadorned. The result is a bloated imagination, sickly judgment and disgust towards all the real businesses of life," he wrote. If it wasn't actual, it wasn't worthwhile, believed our greatest philosopher-president. Imagination became truth's antithesis, even its enemy. Common sense, taken to an irrational extreme.

Common-sense philosophy had spanned two continents, several languages, a flock of conflicting religious and political convictions, and two revolutionary wars. Like a game of telephone, wherein a message is whispered from one person to the next until it's garbled, common sense had come to represent itself, its opposite, its inverse, converse, and contrapositive, and none of the above. It had done yeoman's work representing the common folk, whoever they were and whatever they wanted, but like most yeomen, common sense was denied its proper place of honor: the Constitution of the United States. Achieved by consensus with the goal of ensuring the commonweal, the Constitution's sage federal system of checks and balances between the national government and the states, and within the national government among the executive, legislative and judicial branches, is an everlasting monument to the common sense upon which this nation was founded, yet the Constitution writers never included the expression, by then hopelessly distorted and vagabond.

The CS Devil's Advocate

Since the dawn of the nineteenth century, few philosophers have argued that common sense forms the basis for a coherent belief system. Rather, it is mostly a philosophical devil's advocate, stronger, as Reid originally conceded, in refutation than in confirmation. Some thinkers have welcomed the reality check but most have regarded the common-sense devil's advocate as nothing more than an antiphilosophy that pokes holes, exasperates, and stymies legitimate intellectual inquiry.

Immanuel Kant reviled common sense as "one of the subtlest inventions of modern times, by which the emptiest talker may coolly confront the profoundest thinker, and hold out against him." Yet who could resist taunting the great German metaphysician, considering the scenario he posed in "On a Supposed Right to Tell Lies from Benevolent Motives" (1797). It is late at night and someone pounds hysterically at the door. It is your friend, desperately frightened and pleading to be let in. A killer is chasing her, and so you quickly let her in and lock the door behind you and turn off the lights. A few moments later, a brute carrying a bloody hatchet bangs loudly and demands to know if a woman fitting the description of your friend is inside. Through the peephole you can see a hatchet in his hand and bloodlust in his eyes. Do you tell the truth?

Of course not. Unless, that is, you are one of history's great thinkers. Kant prescribes the truth, the whole truth and nothing but the truth, even though a lie might seem the safest and most humane course of action. Kant finds himself duty bound by the "categorical imperative," which states: "Act only on that maxim through which you can at the same time will that it should become a universal law"—that is, no exceptions. Kant suggests that maybe while you are rationally explaining the situation to the frothing madman, your friend could slip out the back door. But morality, Kant counters, the means by which "we make ourselves worthy of happiness", demands that the axe murderer be told his quarry is inside.

Kant is *mostly* right in his insistence that we should tell the truth and hold firm to universal moral principles. But common sense says that in some situations you do what you have to do to stay alive, theories and categorical imperatives be damned.

G. W. F. Hegel, who believed that the world's soul progressively contradicts itself in order to manifest the divine, had even less regard than Kant did for common sense. In *The Phenomenology of Mind* (1807), Hegel dismisses common sense (*Menschenverstand*) as a trivial, empty abstraction, "a rhetorical melange of commonplace truths." The Teutonic absolute idealist certainly defies common wisdom in the "Lordship and Bondage" section, where he argues beyond a shadow of a doubt that in the master–slave relationship, the slave is superior to the master because the master depends on the slave for his identity, but the slave has no corresponding need to define himself in terms of his owner. The noble intent of Hegel's argument, made at the time when slavery still flourished, is unexceptionable. But benighted old common sense might still say that between the two choices, go with the lordship and deal with the guilt.

For the same reasons that it's easier to be a critic than an artist, a pundit than a politician, common-sense criticisms of philosophical arguments have their limitations. Lying when you have to and lording rather than being lorded over may be commonsensical from time to time but they do not a rigorous moral code make. Just as the universal prescriptions of formal philosophy inevitably clash with practical reality, CS morality frequently leads to inconsistent and self-serving behavior.

Whatever its logical shortcomings, common sense never ceased to be a lively and useful fount of sayings, maxims and the like: "Don't be idle, plan your daily activities, send your children to school, stay on the farm, avoid hard liquor, watch every penny, mend your fences, and be good to your wife," was the kind of common-sense advice offered by *The Old Farmer's Almanac* and scores of competitors on both sides of the Atlantic. "Do not permit a servant to carry a candle to his bedroom if he sleeps in an unplastered garret," or "Do nothing in great haste except catching fleas and running from a mad dog," were among the most helpful reminders.

Because it depends so much on individual interpretation, the inconsistencies of common sense made it seem much more democratic than traditional, "prethought" philosophies. Though increasingly snubbed by professional philosophers, the first half of the nineteenth century was the heyday of common-sense thinking. "Nothing astonishes men so much as common sense and plain dealing," wrote Ralph Waldo Emerson in *Heroism* (1841), his classic study of what it takes to be a mensch. According to Lewis David Simpson in his study of the common-sense tradition in American literature, Emerson, Hawthorne, Melville, and their followers extolled the common-sense virtues of old-fashioned brainpower, Yankee ingenuity, and American knowhow until Thoreau was blue in the face: "A true account of the actual is the rarest poetry, for common sense always takes a hasty and superficial view," retorted the devil's advocate of dreamy living. Henry David Thoreau and his band of rebellious romantics believed that science, the hot new intellectual vogue, was as exciting as poetry and metaphysics and would leave beribboned old common sense in the dust by the side of the road.

The Common-Sense–Science Grudge Match

The Civil War, which rang down the American era of common-sense thinking, was itself an act in the Industrial Revolution. Over the first half of the nineteenth century in England and Europe, and here in the decades after the war ended in 1865, a transcultural metamorphosis brought unprecedented bloodshed, unequaled bounty, undreamt freedom, cataclysmic dislocation, and wholesale abandonment of an agrarian way of life that had remained essentially unchanged since hunter-gatherers roamed. A seemingly timeless body of common knowledge was made obsolete within an average lifetime, which, incidentally, was on its way to doubling, as a result. If the question, "Whatever happened to common sense?" seems appropriate today, back then it stuck like a fork in the eye.

Isaac Newton was responsible. Common sense from Aristotle on down said that for objects to keep moving, you had to keep pushing them; a sack of potatoes would not move across the floor by itself. But Newton discovered that a body in motion remained in motion unless some force, in this case friction, was exerted to stop it. Donald Norman explains in *The Design of Everyday Things* (1989), "Of course, Newton and his successors assume the absence of friction and air. Aristotle lived in a world where there was always friction and air resistance. Once friction is involved, then objects in motion tend to stop unless you keep pushing. Aristotle's theory may be bad physics, but it describes reasonably well what we can see in the real world." Though Newton's discoveries bore little on what normally is, they revolutionized what could be. The decoding of nature's mechanisms enabled creation of humanmade mechanisms, machines to do the work for us. Instead of slave labor separating by hand cotton balls from seeds, the physical work was gradually taken over by Eli Whitney's cotton gin.

Science had wrought these changes, and so science, it followed, would provide the explanations for their new way of life. But what was science, exactly, and how did it relate to common sense? Estimates ranged from completely different to totally superior. "The notion that science has an independent logic of its own is due to the vision of Newton and Descartes—that is, science's purpose is to discover the mental errors of 'common-sense' observations," writes Rafael Lopez-Pintor of the University of Madrid. A touch more charitably, Thomas Henry Huxley, a biologist and educator who was one of Charles Darwin's principal exponents, considered common sense the ape from which science gloriously descends.

In 1868, Huxley wrote, "Science is nothing but trained and organized common sense, differing from the latter only as a veteran may differ from a raw recruit: and its methods differ from those of common sense only as far as the guardsman's cut and thrust differ from the manner in which a savage wields his club." Of course, there were the doubters, naysayers, and loyal common-sense defenders: "Science is a first-rate piece of furniture for a man's upper-chamber, if he has common-sense on the ground floor," Oliver Wendell Holmes warned in 1872, in *The Poet at the Breakfast-Table*. But the way science was going, you might not need a ground floor.

From Social Darwinism to scientific socialism, science was steadily replacing common sense in the affections and affectations of midcentury intellectuals. In Europe, the great revolutionary year 1848 saw the rise of Marxism, the first major political theory explicitly based on perceived scientific principles. Not only was science the intellectual basis for the Industrial

Revolution, it was also the basis for the political system that sprang up to combat its excesses. Much as "common sense" justified the arguments of both sides in the American Revolution, "science" became the universal rallying cry.

Common sense had become a stigma to be avoided. Emile Durkheim, the founder of modern sociology, argued firmly that (1) science is distinct from common sense, and (2) sociology is a science. The left-leaning proponent of collective social thinking and social justice practiced what he preached by applying the empirical and quantitative methods of physical science—as Twain might have put it, the "lies, damned lies and statistics"—to the study of society. Durkheim believed that the essential elements of culture and social structure are internalized by individuals, including sociologists, as part of their personalities. The boundary between the individual and society was not nearly as distinct as the physical boundary between body and environment. Therefore, what individuals might regard as their own commonsensical perspectives on the world were just personal interpretations of the general social values. Thus, sociologists had to be objective, scientific observers, mindful of the viewpoints and prejudices with which society had imbued them.

In "Commonsense, Science and Public Opinion," sociologist Martin Roiser of Ealing College in London, boasts that with today's public opinion surveys and polls, "scientific approaches to studying social phenomena have, over time, replaced commonsense ones, and . . . science now dominates common sense." Though skeptics observe that opinion surveys can be biased by the phrasing of the questions, the self-knowledge and candor of the respondents, the sample sizes, and the statistical evaluation techniques, it is indeed a fitting testament to the field that nowadays almost everyone, critic and proponent, thinks sociology has escaped common sense completely.

Originally, common-sense philosophy arose to oppose the seventeenth-century skeptic's belief that ideas are all that exist, or at least all that we can be sure of. By the end of the nineteenth century, however, common sense was being challenged with the opposite conviction, that everything could be known. What had changed most in the debate was the role of the senses: from fallible, possibly universally deceptive human organs, to the best source of knowledge about the world, particularly when amplified by technological instruments such as microscopes and telescopes. With industrialization a new generation of facts, statistics, and other scientific data asserted their claims to the truth like so many unknown heirs turning up with ironclad wills.

Just as common sense had absorbed revolutionary new discoveries in the past—the earth going from flat to round, for example—it might also have coopted the Industrial Revolution and regained its intellectual bearings. But then physics returned in the form of Einstein et al., and sent common sense spinning like a runaway globe.

$$E = CS^2$$

Let's say that you are to be honored with a star-studded gala hosted by the Rockefeller family at their Center, and that you don't know your way around New York City. What information do you need? The avenue (the General Electric building is best approached from Fifth, cross streets, Forty-ninth and Fiftieth) and the floor (just ask for the Rainbow Room). There you have your three dimensions, the x-, y-, and z-axes that high-school geometry taught are necessary to locate any point in space. Still, there's something else you need to know: When, at what time? The t-axis. The day before yesterday?

The *Times* of London once referred to Einstein's relativity theory, which proposes an "*x, y, z, t*" space–time continuum and suggests the potential for travel through time, as "an affront to common sense." But in fact it is the purest common sense. First broached in 1905, then expanded in 1911, Einstein's realization that time is the fourth dimension, and that every "thing" is actually an event, is a premise everyone can grasp. That a house is not only an object but even more essentially, an event— a coming together of labor and material at a specific time and lasting a specific time. The same for a tree, a person, a rock, a planet—all events, albeit of widely varying durations. Common sense, post-Einstein, says the universe is made up of events, not things.

"The whole of science is nothing more than a refinement of everyday thinking," wrote Einstein. Where the greatest physicist since Newton made his immortal refinement was to ask himself not just about events common to this plane of existence, but at microcosmic and macrocosmic extremes. In Bronowski's re-creation, Einstein wondered what he would see if he sat on an electron traveling at the speed of light. His answer, published in the same year as the special theory of relativity (1905), was the beginning of quantum theory, specifically a study of the photoelectric effect, for which he eventually won the Nobel prize. The bad news for common sense was that the subatomic building blocks of our existence are made up of events utterly bizarre.

Imagine two identical cue balls made at the same time and from the same block of ivory; one ends up in a pool hall in Sandusky, Ohio, and the other is smuggled onto the Pacific island of Fiji. Were they to act like a quantum pair of subatomic particles, the moment the Ohio cue ball was shot and sent spinning clockwise the Fiji ball would be observed to be spinning counterclockwise at exactly the same rate! And vice versa—if the Fiji ball were shot, a player in Sandusky would instantly observe that her cue ball was rotating in an equal, opposite manner.

Common sense can only shudder in amazement at this thought experiment, the Einstein-Podolsky-Rosen electron-pair paradox. But quantum theory clearly implies that if two sub-atomic particles are created in a collision, the moment the spin of one member of that particle pair is determined by observation, the other member of that pair, no matter how far away it is, even all the way across the universe, will instantaneously—faster than the speed of light—go from an indeterminate state to one in which its spin is known to be exactly equal and opposite to the spin of its mate. Though offered by Einstein as a challenge to quantum orthodoxy, the doctrine of instantaneous nonlocal causation has been confirmed by theoretical physicists David Bohm and, later, J. S. Bell.

Bertrand Russell explains, "Modern physics is further from common sense than the physics of the nineteenth century. It has dispensed with matter, substituting a series of events; it has abandoned continuity in microscopic phenomena; and it has substituted statistical averages for strict deterministic causality affecting each individual occurrence" (*Human Knowledge: Its Scope and Limits,* 1948). Thus, it turns out that Berkeley was a lot closer than Johnson to the physical truth of the matter in their stone-kicking controversy. Twentieth-century physics holds that stones and all other objects are indeed composed of arcane subatomic events, many of which have never been physically detected but only theorized thus far—they are only ideas. Johnson's toe must be throbbing in its grave.

Common sense might still say the heck with all these wild ideas, no matter how many luminaries espouse them, but atomic weaponry, generations of communications, and information technology developed from quantum theory say otherwise.

Modern Art Couldn't Help It

Since the days of the Neolithic cave paintings at Altamira and Lascaux, artists had been in the business of representing reality. It was a great service to re-create a historical scene, a vista of natural beauty, a famous person's characteristic look. Then in the nineteenth century along came photography, and the art of representing reality gradually became a picture-perfect science. The eye no longer had to be interpreted by the hand, threatening to put a lot of artistic hands out of business. The art world responded by seeing the inner, the other, the Cubist essence, the whatever didn't look like what technology could do better.

The Impressionists responded to this competition with textbook perfection, going technology one better by capturing depth and beauty forever beyond the range of the lens; the artist's interpretive role grew, though not to the point of distortion. Common sense says art should be beautiful, but maybe Monet, Renoir, Degas, Manet and the other Impressionists did such an immortally magnificent job that artists who followed them felt their only choice was to rebel against beauty.

But DADA? The doctrineless doctrine of creative anarchy decided that art was all about getting a response, even a hostile one. Marcel Duchamp hung an upside-down urinal in a Paris art gallery, designed a collection of machines whose purpose was not to work, penciled in a mustache and dirty words on a print of the Mona Lisa, and was hailed as creative genius. After DADA came surrealism. Freud's dreamwork gone visual was the motif. André Breton, the self-proclaimed founder, declared surrealism the "revolution of the unconscious." Problem was that most of the unconscious revolutionaries had psyches filled with lamprey eels. Did German surrealist Max Ernst ever get a peaceful night's sleep? Only Salvador Dalí really seemed to have fun with it all, with those great drippy watches. But to the casual onlooker, a Jackson Pollock painting is like common sense thrown up on its shirt.

Sometimes art seemed like a genius conspiracy to screw things up. Piet Mondrian figured out how to draw lots of straight lines that, if you looked closely, made the spaces between them go crooked. Arnold Schoenberg must have spent years researching the precise tonal combinations that send chills spearing up and down the human spine. James Joyce, perhaps the most esteemed English-language writer of the twentieth century, filled his masterpieces with streams of nonsense. "All profoundly original art looks ugly at first," declared art historian Clement Greenberg, summarizing the triumphant new aesthetic, without a bit of irony. To the innocent CS bystander, the greatest creative flowering since the Renaissance also seemed like history's most colossal practical joke.

Primary truths? First principles? In the first half of the twentieth century, philosophers dropped common-sense pragmatism like a dead cat. Common sense said common sense was no way to describe the new reality. The only loyalist was G. E. Moore, a beloved Cambridge professor who beguiled his students and peers with aphorisms such as "Whenever a philosopher says something is really real, you can be really sure that what he says is 'really real' isn't real, really." Moore's strategy for defending common sense was to split the idea into two definitions: sometimes it simply meant universal beliefs, at other times it meant those beliefs which people are, by nature, inclined to hold. The so-called universals can change from epoch to epoch, say, from

Agrarian Age to Industrial Revolution to Information Age, but the natural beliefs are more lasting.

Moore relativized common sense, arguing that common-sense beliefs are weighted by certainty. Some beliefs, such as that water exists, are so heavily weighted that dissent seems impossible. Others—say, that camels can travel long distances across the desert on little water—are certain enough only to inhibit dissent, but not preclude it. Any belief to which reasonable objections can be raised, such as that camels can get all the water they need from dates, is beyond the pale of common sense, whether or not it is correct. How common sense had fallen! Unlike Reid, who arrogantly declared his common sense to be the philosophy of first principles that everyone just naturally knew, the most Moore could offer up was the polite defense that common sense actually exists. Moore's gentleman philosophy never really made it past World War II, and today his work on common sense is usually dismissed or ignored.

The German-American philosopher Hannah Arendt wrote common-sense philosophy's postwar epitaph in "Understanding and Politics: On the Nature of Totalitarianism" (1951): "Since the beginning of this century, the growth of meaninglessness has been accompanied by a loss of common sense. In many respects, this has appeared simply as an increasing stupidity." Arendt, who had fled the Nazis at the start of the war and whose distinguished analysis of the "banality of evil" captured the essence of the War Crimes tribunal at Nuremberg, saw the modern world as one "where the most commonly accepted ideas have been 'attacked, refuted, surprised and dissolved by facts' and where therefore we witness a 'kind of insolvency of imagination and bankruptcy of understanding.' "

Anti-Common Sense

The CS low point of the twentieth century may have been reached in China during Mao Zedong's Cultural Revolution, when not only political murder—known as the Deprivation of Existence campaign, in which more than twenty million persons were exterminated for their political beliefs—but political cannibalism became the preferred means for showing one's loyalty. Fighting to devour strips of flesh from eviscerated lackeys, as recently reported about the Red Guard era, was the way to get ahead.

Beyond the atrocities, the communist assault on common sense was characterized by relentless subversion. Common sense conflicts fundamentally with any attempt to declare reality, or to make it conform to dogma. Consider this line from an old Bolshevik hymn: "We will command the wind and the rain." Taught to three generations of schoolchildren throughout the Soviet bloc, it epitomizes common sense sacrificed for the sake of ideology. The logic of proletarian supremacy said that things *had* to be this way, and therefore they were, and not only in words. While researching an article on postcommunist economics for *The New York Times Magazine,* I learned that throughout the Soviet sphere corn, a lowland crop, was sometimes planted in the mountains, and cattle were grazed on grassless lands. Because that was the Plan.

Josef Stalin had a simple approach to uncooperative realities—fiction. Irked that the West was producing so many more great inventions than the Soviet bloc, which by ironclad Marxist-Leninist rationale must surpass the capitalists, Stalin commissioned a team of scholars to hasten the inevitable and invent some inventors. Making up biographies was easy, the august team found, but what had happened to all the great inventions? *Great Russian Inventors,* published around 1950, became the big book of great, and terribly unfortunate, Russian inventors. Each story ended in a mysterious tragedy. I'll bet you didn't know that an unsung Soviet genius invented the most awesome tank in history—could have cut through Hitler's Panzers like a can opener—but, as luck would have it, the tank was so huge and powerful that it sank into a marsh, never to be seen again. . . .

Sometimes it seemed as though the communists' strategy was to assault common sense head on, not unlike the way armies psychologically break down their recruits, punishing them without reason, purposefully not making sense in order to disorient and subjugate. Unlike the army, however, most communist regimes had no intention or program to build their subjects back up to self-esteem. *Slum Clearance,* a 1987 play by Václav Havel, dramatizes the true, absurd story of the bureaucratic decision to tear down a beautiful old church at the center of the town of Liberec, Czechoslovakia. The ostensible reason was to make way for more workers' housing which, as everyone knew from the start, would never be built. The real reason, according to the drama, went even beyond destroying the church as a symbol of forbidden religion. The demolition was done precisely because it made no sense, demonstrating the utter power of the government, and the abject powerlessness of the people over their own lives. Common sense was not only the victim, but the enemy.

6

Is There a Common-Sense Culture?

Yes, But It's Iceland

"Common sense is knowing how not to harm that which you are trying to help. It comes from experience, and includes the ability to improvise," says Vigdís Finnbogadóttir, president of the nation of Iceland, after she considers my question with a thoughtful pause. With queenly bearing she has come to Washington, D.C., in October 1991 to address the national press corps to celebrate the 1,000th anniversary of Leif Ericson's discovery of Vinland, now known as North America. Just as Leif Ericson Day is October 9, the week before Columbus Day, this commemoration was held in 1991, the year before the 500th anniversary of Columbus's 1492 voyage; Leif got there first, was the not-so-subtle point.

In 1980, Vigdís, as her constituents call her, became the first woman in world history to be popularly elected head of state; she has since been reelected three times by overwhelming majorities, including 1992, when she ran unopposed. It's easy to see why. I asked this former director of the Icelandic National Theatre (though never an actress, she is quick to point out) if she

could recall having exercised any of the common-sense helpful-
ness that she described.

Vigdís responded with the story of Gudrídur Thorbjarnar-
dóttir, one of the best-traveled women in the medieval world.
Gudrídur, granddaughter of a liberated Irish house slave, was
rescued from a shipwreck by Leif. She soon married Leif's
brother Thorsteinn and then crossed the North Atlantic with
their Viking crew. They appear to have settled somewhere between Newfoundland and Boston, calling their new home Vinland, Land of Grapes, a.k.a. Land of Wine. There Thorsteinn
was killed by natives, and so Gudrídur married the merchant
Thorfinnur Karlsefni and gave birth to the boy Snorri, the first
European child born on our continent. After three years in
Vinland, she sailed back to Iceland, raised her family, and was
eventually widowed again. Gudrídur, who had adopted Christianity when Leif Ericson did, was nonetheless renowned for the
beauty with which she sang ancient pagan songs. Accompanied
only by her angelic voice and undoubted skill with the sword,
she made a penitential pilgrimage to Rome, mostly on foot.
Eventually she returned to northern Iceland to build a church
and become the country's first abbess.

Hard to argue that Gudrídur knew how to get along in the
world. Yet usually when someone is asked about whom they
think of as having lots of common sense, at least in my interviewing experience over the past few years, living persons, or
maybe a deceased parent, grandparent, or teacher, comes to
mind. Never some historical figure dead for ten centuries.
Vigdís spoke of Gudrídur fondly, with the sense of familiarity
some people have when they talk about Biblical characters. In
Iceland, the ancient Viking sagas are in many ways more important than the Bible, for they preserve the country's culture and
heritage. American culture has no counterpart, nor most others,

for that matter. Vigdís explains that the sagas give Icelanders their bond of language and history.

"Ours is a living ancient language. We cannot forget our history because we speak very much the same language that our ancestors did a thousand years ago," says Vigdís. Indeed, the Icelandic vocabulary, derived from Old Danish, seems like it has been frozen in time—about 500 of the 520 commonest Icelandic words remain essentially unchanged since Viking days. Merchants, lovers, and children at play use much the same language their counterparts did at the turn of the millennium. As a result, most Icelanders can read the ancient sagas of the twelfth and thirteenth centuries with comparative ease—comparable to understanding Shakespeare's seventeenth-century Early Modern English.

"This unusual continuity is in no small measure the result of the country's almost total isolation for more than half a millennium to the turn of this century," writes Sigurdur Magnússon in *The Icelanders* (1990), to which Vigdís has written the foreword. Magnússon refers to the country's post-Viking "dark ages," which hit their depths in the nineteenth century, when at least a fifth of the population was reduced to begging and vagrancy. The gloom began began to lift with autonomy from Danish rule, won during World War I, and then with independence in 1944, after British and then American military bases opened up Iceland to the rest of the world. Many Icelanders can still recall life before electricity, automobiles, and telephones. This unusually long living memory is possible partly because, along with the Japanese, Icelanders now live longer than any other people in the world.

Genealogy is a national obsession. The philosophy is simple: the more you know about your past, the likelier it is that you will discover a connection with someone else. Scores of private autobiographies are published each year, tracing family history as close as possible to the island's settlement in the year 874. Even today, with population at its peak, the country has only about 250,000 people, with very few immigrants. The patronymic system, in which the father's first name becomes a child's last name, with "-sson" or "-dóttir" attached as appropriate, gives a one-big-family feeling to the culture; telephone directories list people alphabetically by first name. When two Icelanders from different parts of the country meet each other for the first time, it is much more surprising if they don't have an acquaintance or relative in common than if they do.

Icelanders are also united by their battle against the elements, those which descend and those which erupt. Their 40,000-square-mile island is the bulge that happened when the North American and European tectonic plates collided. The problem is that the two vast crustal chunks still shift and rub up against each other, causing earthquakes and, particularly, volcanoes; Iceland accounts for about half of the Earth's eruptions. Whole towns have been engulfed by lava and swamped by poisonous gas; most recently Heimaey, the capital city of the south, had to be entirely evacuated in 1973. The country floats on a sea of hot water—which Vigdís calls Iceland's gold because of its tremendous clean-heating capacity, including the entire city of Reykjavik—spouting up in geysers and hot springs, a steamy reminder that molten lava is not far below.

The story goes that Iceland and Greenland received their respective names in one of history's earliest real-estate scams. Iceland, warmed by the Gulf Stream, is unexpectedly green and thus was dubbed icy by settlers who wanted to keep their find secret; calling Greenland green was like nicknaming the Sahara "Land o' Lakes." But what Iceland gains from the currents it loses in wind chill, holding records for being one of the windiest places on Earth, with more than 200 gale-force days annually; for having the highest waves, up to 26 meters, or about eight and a half stories of pulverizing North Atlantic surf; and for suffering the northern hemisphere's fiercest winter storms. Huddled together in their very long, very dark winters, Icelanders share everything they have to share.

Clearly, the culture has the "in common" part down, but what about the "sense"? Wouldn't battling all those elements drive you out of your mind? Perhaps Prime Minister David Oddsson, who in nine months went from being the most popular mayor in the history of the capital city of Reykjavik to Iceland's least popular political leader, was the wrong person to ask this question, though not even his legion of critics deny that he has a keen wit. The prime minister battles just for the fun of it, and with his unruly shock of curly black hair, meathook hands, and stubby frame, plays beast to Vigdís's beauty. At a United Nations luncheon in New York, I asked Oddsson to define the Icelandic version of common sense: "Common sense—let me see, I guess the way we say that is 'healthy mind.' I would say that common sense is what the head of a family naturally has, or has to have in order for his family to stay healthy. In Iceland the environment forces you to have common sense, or else you will be in trouble. The same in politics. Too much book learning can be destructive." How does the environment cause people to have common sense? By killing them if they don't, seems to be the answer.

Icelanders are a seafaring folk, and with three-quarters of the gross national product coming out of the stormy North Atlantic, it takes risk and hard work to earn each crown (worth about two cents). When the adversary is Nature, hatred has no part in the battle. Nature means no harm, or for that matter, no help. Compared to situations where survival depends on

defeating other people, the battle against the elements is unsul-
lied by regret, guilt, untoward desire. (It's like the difference in
psyches between policemen and firemen; the latters' enemy is
deadly but not evil, and their duty is relatively uncomplicated by
politics and moral dilemmas.) It's a much cleaner game—you
against the ocean, the winds, the cold. This climate, meteoro-
logical and psychological, is uniquely conducive to common-
sense thinking. At least that was my theory. When I tried it out
on Iceland's leaders, both good cop and bad cop gave the same
sly smile and suggested that I visit and see for myself. I did, late
in August 1992, to see what common sense, Icelandic style, is
really all about.

Common Sense, Viking Style

The European and North American continental plates meet and
face each other as two massive stone ridges in a place called
Thingvellir, the magical plain where the world's oldest parliament, the Althing, first met in the year 930. Whatever geo-
magnetic synchronicity it was that drew Iceland's original
thirty-nine chieftains to gather each year at that precise inland
spot, it worked.

"The greatest example of common sense in the history of our
nation came in the year 1000, when Christianity was adopted,
without bloodshed or tyranny. I believe that this set a healthy,
pragmatic tone for the nation ever since," says Hanna Maria
Petursdóttir, the priestess and director of the national park
at Thingvellir. She explains that when the Althing peacefully
adopted Christianity as the country's official religion, they
avoided war with the King of Norway, who was intent on
Christianization. With the chieftains' decision came a second,
less formal doctrine. Privately, Icelanders were free to practice
any religion they liked, including the Norse god worship that

was their heritage. Bishops were elected, priests were appointed, churches were built, and Christianity was incorporated into the body of laws. But sacrifices to heathen gods were still carried out at temples in homes. Without a drop of blood, inevitable change and ancient tradition were both accommodated.

Imagine those thirty-nine grizzled Viking leaders sitting around the fire, passing around the jug, and getting the gospel. "Love thine enemy" and "Turn the other cheek," a common-sense stretch for most people, must have seemed like some sort of practical joke. "Thou shalt not steal," might have sounded pretty reasonable at first because stealing, by stealth or trickery, was also against their moral code. But imagine the gnarly chieftains' confusion upon finding out that robbery was forbidden too! Up-front, in-your-face, I'll-take-it-because-I-can robbery was not only legit in the Viking code, it gave their lifestyle that special zing. On balance, common sense told them that it was probably worth the trouble of accepting the Bible, for all its wimpy rules, rather than having the King of Norway rain his holy hell upon their island. Unless, of course, this whole turn-the-other-cheek business turned out to be some sort of diabolical plot to catch them off guard. Here the ancient wisdom of *Hávamál*, the store of Viking sayings, provided a trusty reminder:

> Be your friend's
> true friend.
> Return gift for gift.
> Repay laughter
> with laughter again
> but betrayal with treachery.

The gods almost managed to put the kibosh on Christianity but their aim was a little off, according to Jonas Kristjansson, director of Reykjavik's Arne Magnússon Institute, where ancient saga scrolls are kept in bombproof, climate-controlled underground vaults. The first time Christian priests sang mass at the Althing a tremendous volcanic eruption sounded to the west. The lava of the coming of Christianity, as it is still known, engulfed the farm of one of the chieftains, who pointed angrily to the white-robed priests and declared, "No wonder the gods are angry when they hear such heathen speeches!" and suggested tossing the Christian troublemakers into the lava. But another chieftain, Snorri (not Gudrídur's boy and not yet Christian) retorted that the very spot where they stood had once been burned by lava, and so the gods must also have been angry then. Snorri's argument was not idealistic or humanitarian, just that it didn't make sense to wreck a perfectly good political agreement just because some volcano erupts somewhere.

"Icelanders are noted for their lack of principles for the very simple reason that the concept 'principle' does not exist in their language. This curious fact probably tells something about their pragmatic and utilitarian relationship to reality and their down-to-earth instinct for survival. This instinct was memorably demonstrated in the year 1000, when Christianity was peacefully adopted by the Althing (Parliament) in a predominantly pagan and warlike society, an outstanding example of political compromise aimed at preserving the nation's peace and unity. In a sense the whole history of the Icelanders is evidence of this indomitable survival instinct in a hostile environment, where the blind forces of nature were the principal adversary and questions of principles were secondary, if at all pertinent," writes Magnússon. In other words, if the gods had shot their angry lava closer to the mark, the evening's entertainment would have been priests flambés.

Icelanders have a saying that common sense (*allmen skynsemi*) is cheap, true intelligence rare. They are about the least likely people to analyze things to death. For a nation that leads the world in per capita book consumption, even at the exorbitant price of $50 per hardcover, you see little in the way of philosophy, psychology, or sociology. The literature that tides readers over those excruciatingly long, dark winters is poetry, epic, biography, adventure, stories of all sorts—food for the imagination, not the intellect. (Much of the culture's analytical urge is spent on chess, a game of intellectual warfare. More grand masters per capita live in Iceland than anywhere else, and chess stories are a standard part of the evening sports news.)

"Public opinion is seldom a lie," goes a bit of popular wisdom. From Viking times on down, good name and reputation have been far more important than strict personal integrity. Iceland is an example of the entity anthropologist Ruth Benedict calls a "shame culture," as opposed to a "guilt culture." In her classic study of Japanese society, *The Chrysanthemum and the Rose,* Benedict contends that in "guilt" cultures, as found in most Christian countries, including the United States, codes of conduct are based on questions of intrinsic right and wrong and stem primarily from an individual's relationship with God, or with his or her own internal standards. In "shame cultures," such as Japan and, Magnusson persuasively argues, Iceland, society, not conscience, is the judge. Values are contingent; the orientation is less toward principles than appearances—whether or not you get caught. The "guilt" system's escape valve is unburdening by religious confession or psychotherapy. But such talking cures are not possible in a "shame" culture, for the whole idea is to save face and keep things secret.

Shame cultures do, however, have their own hundred-proof formula for letting down hair. In Tokyo, snootful salary-men weave their way home secure in the knowledge that if they told off their bosses, confessed some liaison, or were other-wise woefully indiscreet, it was all within bounds because they were drunk, a sufficient excuse. In Reykjavik, fashion-forward throngs of very young adults surge like rugby scrums, emitting bottles, fistfights and delirious screams. Whatever this Viking thing is, it comes back with a vengeance when liquor is served. Icelanders of both sexes drink to get drunk and get drunk to act like Vikings, which is to say bang some heads, sing some songs, and have some sex. The women sometimes skip the head bang-ing. Of his fellow Icelanders, Magnússon confirms that "in a drunken state they *are* Vikings."

Common sense, Viking style, says that alcohol is a means to an end—the end of sobriety. A great apocryphal story is about three Icelandic boys who found a bottle of fine French wine. Great hooch, but not enough for all of them to get drunk. They poured it into a bucket and stuck their feet in the wine, so that the alcohol would be absorbed into the blood vessels between their toes. "Common sense" depends on your priorities.

The Scandinavian Rogue

The morning-after consequences of neo-Viking revelry extend far beyond furry tongues. More than one third of Icelandic children are born out of wedlock, often to mothers who are quite young. Yet most of these children are raised by both parents; that a father will support and care for his child is, in Iceland, a social given. Marriage, in this post-heathen culture, is an optional ceremony. And, by the way, the taxes that drive up the price of the alcoholic beverages that got the ball rolling in the first place go to pay for programs of national health care (free to everyone) and education (free up to the university level, for which one pays about $500 a year).

If there's any more sensible investment than taking good care of the kids in the first place, rather than paying for it tenfold later on, I'd like to know about it. Icelanders have that wonderful Scandinavian attitude toward children, that they are the most precious creatures in the world. Every culture prides itself on the way its children are cared for, but none surpasses the gentle, loving manner and comprehensive social-welfare system that Scandinavians provide for their young. Everyone acts like a parent when young children are around, watching out for them, picking them up and brushing them off if they fall, quietly encouraging or admonishing them. Throughout the region it is socially unacceptable, and in some countries illegal, for an adult to slap or even speak harshly to a child.

(Over the years several Scandinavian friends have mentioned that one of the most uncomfortable aspects of traveling to other countries, including the United States, is seeing parents punish their children, sometimes corporally, in public. They are too polite, or shocked, to mention the recent revelation that after twelve years of "family values" administrations, the United States ranked behind every state in the Americas except Haiti and Bolivia in vaccinating children against polio and other childhood diseases!)

Three factors help explain the Scandinavian priority on child care. The first is cultural, the commonality argument, which holds that people care more for their neighbors and for their neighbors' children when they all share heritage and traits. The second is economic, that children have traditionally been considered more of an asset in sparsely populated societies, where labor is scarce, and more of a liability in overcrowded societies, where resources are scarce. Thus, the theory goes, the loving attitude that prevails in Scandinavia, which has only about one-ninth the population density of neighboring western Europe. (At only six persons per square mile, Iceland is lower by far than Finland, Sweden, Denmark or Norway, the next sparsest at about thirty.) A third explanation is that Scandinavian children receive the attention they do because their mothers have such a powerful political voice in government.

"In seafaring cultures, women have always had a higher status because the men had to rely on them so heavily to take care of the house, family, business affairs," said Vigdís, explaining that from the days of the Vikings, who sailed as far south as the Saudi peninsula, and west to North America, on down to present-day fishermen, who can spend weeks at a time on giant factory ships, Icelandic men have always spent long stretches at sea, leaving the women no choice but to manage home and community. Today, Icelandic women account for almost a third of municipal and regional offices, and about a fifth of seats in the Althing. Half that share is held by the Women's Alliance, a political party formed as the result of a national strike by women in October 1975, the largest mass gathering in Iceland's history.

Scandinavians are bleeding-heart liberals in their racial politics and attitudes, and proud of it. Each year Norwegian high-school students participate in a national program in which they put in more than one million hours of community service (quite a lot considering that the Norwegian population is only four million). The millions of dollars in wages that they would have received are instead donated to a charitable organization, selected by a government panel, which runs environmental and educational programs in the Third World. The students get the experience, the community gets the service, the Third World gets the aid it needs, and Norway builds an international image ten times its size, and pricelessly positive. Icelandic culture has similar liberal racial attitudes, though in less sophisticated form than its Scandinavian big brothers.

"The little kids would all run up to me and try to rub the color off. I would just pick them up and smile," says Nebraska Franklin III, a seventeen-year-old black high-school student from Chicago's South Side, who for his first trip outside the inner city spent summer 1991 in Iceland as an American Field Service exchange student. Franklin recalls that the senior citizens found him just as much of a novelty, and would pass their mornings watching the young black man run and swim. "It was nothing negative, just curiosity. It was fine by me," says Franklin.

Odds are that the children, at least, will meet many more individuals of different background and color. More than half of Icelanders travel abroad each year, a particularly astonishing number given that to leave the country one must cross the North Atlantic; They have no equivalent of driving back and forth across the Canadian or Mexican border to pump up the travel stats. Travel builds common sense by forcing the traveler to handle practical matters in unfamiliar circumstances and to improvise from the available resources. It's another way of testing one's mettle against the world. Balancing off Icelandic culture's unique, almost incubated commonality is the equally important shared experience of venturing beyond.

"Icelanders like people with guts. They're like Americans in how much they value initiative," said American-born Leo Kolbeinsson, the first foreigner ever elected to head an Icelandic trade union, a league of small shopkeepers. Kolbeinsson's adopted countrymen have that gung-ho free enterprise can-do attitude that sets them apart from many of their Scandinavian cousins, particularly the socialist Swedes. In Iceland, when somebody says he's built his house, he doesn't mean he "had it built," as in "We're building a house down at the shore." He means he built it with his own labor and probably got lots of help from friends. In Sweden such ambition might incur serious legal consequences—helping a neighbor in even so small a task as building a fence is a reportable crime if the appropriate wages and *taxes* are not paid.

Of community *über alles* Sweden it has been said that boredom is the national sickness. In rogue and peasant Iceland, eccentricity is the plague—the island is overrun by characters, comedians, crooners and hams. It was about 2:00 A.M. at a country dance in the far northern town of Saudur Krokur (population 1,500), when my hosts Oli and Vigfus insisted that I accompany them to the men's room. Inside the lavatory, taking advantage of the acoustics, the local farmers' choir had assembled to harmonize a medley of traditional songs. Out came the mentholated snuff, around went the vodka, and pretty soon the choir, which now included any man ready to sing, emerged and took over the ballroom stage. They sounded better in the bathroom, but common sense, Icelandic style, says give it a try and so what if you end up looking a little stupid. That's entertaining too.

Common Sense, Natural and Supernatural

As the world's only technologically advanced hunter-gatherer society, some things that are common sense in Iceland may seem cruel and unusual to other cultures. Yet perhaps more than any other, it balances the needs of nature and humankind.

In Heimaey, capital and only populated island of the Westman archipelago, youngsters unsupervised except by each other dart about until the wee morning hours late in August and early in September, with the single-minded mission of capturing baby puffins and putting them into boxes. Puffins, black and white plumaged, look like snubnosed toucans, and toward the end of each summer, thousands of these tiny clown-faced fledglings lose their way at night and end up on Heimaey's docks and streets, where they risk being crushed, eaten by cats, dying from exposure, and so on. It's the (human) children to the rescue, giving their puffin counterparts a good night's food and shelter, releasing them in the morning. Of course, all this running around builds up an appetite, perhaps for a late-night snack of smoked (adult) puffin, which tastes like a cross between smoked duck and bluefish, or maybe a hearty puffin-egg breakfast omelette.

"We take from two stages of the bird's life cycle, never three, never the babies. This way we get what we need while preserving the species," says Captain Hjalmar Gudnason, explaining that the practice helps preserve the puffin population, about six million throughout the archipelago. It also serves as a good object lesson for the children that the prey species must be preserved.

Hunters and fishermen understand that they are not the only predators in the ecological chain. Unchecked by hunting, the puffins, along with the millions of other birds swirling about the islands, would consume even greater quantities of fish. But Gudnason points out that the real competition comes from the whales. From the fishermen's perspective, the current international ban on commercial whaling is like forbidding farmers to stop foxes from entering the henhouse. Although most of

Iceland's gross national product comes from the fishing industry, overfishing by mammals, human and cetacean, has caused industry catch quotas to plummet. Once on the verge of extinction, particularly the larger species, whales have multiplied since receiving protection, on average eating as much fish daily as a thousand persons might.

Particularly in Iceland, the job of common sense is to deal with whatever nature dishes out. In June 1973, Mt. Eldfell erupted, right in the capital city of Heimaey. The archipelago's entire 4,900 population had to be evacuated immediately. As the torrents of lava burned home after home and threatened to close off the harbor for good, an idea at once sensible and outrageous saved the day. Spray seawater on the lava to cool it down and keep it from engulfing the capital city. At first this task seemed every bit as mammoth as holding back the tides, but brigades were formed and hoses were manned, and the lava, as Heimaey residents delight in showing, was checked. And the harbor, with its natural new breakwater, was vastly improved.

Nature can also stand common sense on its head, as in November 1963, when the sea began to boil. That was the day when the island of Surtsey rose out of the ocean, a giant black column spouting lava and lightning and seawater steam. Surtsey, which erupted intermittently for almost five years, is considered the world's youngest island and has been permanently protected as an ecological research preserve, which, after a year's wangling, I got permission to visit.

"You see these boulders, how smooth they are? The geologists used to believe that it took many millions of years to get them so smooth. But now we know they are made instantly, when big drops of lava fall into the cold ocean water," said my guide Snorri Oskarsson as we clambered over great piles of oval black boulders, very smooth and slippery when wet. "If these are made in only an instant, and whole islands are created in a matter of months and years, what need is there for multi-million-year evolutionary theories?" Snorri's creationist geology was a blast from the past, almost like a flat-earth argument. Completely wrong, according to the past few centuries of earth science, yet perfectly consonant with the realities of his environment.

Icelanders are a hard bunch to tell things to. They would much rather be wrong sticking to their guns than wrong going along with someone else's idea. Take the issue of elves. Iceland is the only nation, with the possible exception of blood-related Ireland, where it is possible to get into a full-blown argument with intelligent adults over the existence of elves. Maybe it's a holdover from the ancient paganism that, as we saw, was not banned when the Althing accepted Christianity. Maybe it's because the winters are so long and dark that figments of the imagination scamper through the shadows. Maybe the blasted creatures really exist! Throughout the countryside are roads that had to be detoured and glens left untouched for no other reason than that these creatures ostensibly reside there. Far better to be wrong defending the existence of elves, gnomes and other (presumably) mythical creatures than to admit the illogic of the belief, and then be the victim of some devilish revenge. When it comes to the supernatural, Icelandic common sense says, why take the chance?

"I do not believe in elves. But I do believe in the stories," said the head of state, shifting in her seat. Upon hearing of Vigdis's comments, her constituents empathized with the plight of their leader, recognizing that what she had done she did for the good of the national reputation, and crossing their fingers on her behalf, and their own.

It is possible, however, to go to the elf well once too often. Grettir the Strong, the legendary he-man of the sagas, had a bad habit of killing other men. After one murder, the man's friends asked where he was. Grettir blamed the night troll for the killing, but then someone noticed that it was daytime . . .

Though he says he has no more of it "than eight men in ten," Captain Eirikur Kristofersson, age 100, a short, powerfully built man with a trimmed silver beard, has used common sense in dealing with both the natural and supernatural worlds. Kristofersson is most famous for his clever victory in the 1958 "Cod War." Iceland had just expanded its territorial fishing limits and his job as captain of a Coast Guard cutter was to defend against incursions by the British fleet, which protested against the claim by laying its own territorial buoy markers. Iceland has no armed forces, meaning that Kristofersson was forced to pit his wits against his enemy's firepower. Common sense told him to trust, quite literally, in the wisdom of Solomon. While engaging the admiral of the invading fleet in a Bible-quoting contest over ship-to-ship radio, the wily captain took out his rifle, shot and sank the British buoys, carefully interposing his ship in such a way as to block the sound of the shots from reaching the enemy.

"My quotations were better than his, except for one time he got me with a good one. Fortunately, I am old enough now not to remember which verse it was," said Kristofersson. By the time the British figured out what was going on, diplomacy had taken over, eventually settling the matter in favor of Iceland, possession being nine-tenths of even international law. Because he also managed to save two British sailors swept overboard in another skirmish, Kristofersson was honored not only in his own country but also in Great Britain, which conferred, in the name of Her Majesty Queen Elizabeth II, the honor of "Honorary Commander of the Civil Division of the Order of the British Empire."

Beyond combat heroics, the plaques, awards, press clippings, and books chronicling Kristofersson's achievements that fill his room in a senior citizens' center outside Reykjavik attest to an astonishing record of rescues at sea. When asked about it all, this Icelandic national hero steadfastly maintains that much of the guidance over his illustrious career has come from the spirit world. He points to an illuminated black-and-white photograph of a man with a dark, piercing gaze: Magnus, a friend and physician long deceased, has been his spirit guide since the end of World War II.

Kristofersson's reputation for "seeing and hearing things that other people don't," as he puts it, was made in 1956 when, as captain of a Coast Guard vessel, he suddenly reversed course away from port and headed back into a furious North Atlantic storm. On Magnus's instructions—not a radio message, not any other conventional communication—the captain headed out to a specific set of coordinates several hours out to sea. There Kristofersson found the British ship, *Northern Star,* which, all eight hands confirmed, had been sinking for twelve hours, and which went under several minutes after the last crew member, the captain, was rescued. "At first I did not know where these insights were coming from and I tried to ignore them. But once I understood that it was Magnus speaking, I had no trouble using what I learned," he explained.

Common sense told Kristofersson that there are things in life that ordinary common sense just can't explain. Almost every Icelander I asked knew of someone else, frequently a seafarer, who considered himself to have a relationship akin to

Kristofersson's with Magnus, or to be engaged in a similar form of communication. No one dismissed the notion out of hand. Clearly, common sense can exist, even flourish, in people who hold some very uncommonsensical beliefs. If we had complete and accurate information, would there be logical explanations for all the old sea captain's accomplishments? Or are there times in life when the smartest thing to do is defer to solid results?

7

Where Is Common Sense Going?

Down the World Bank's Tubes

The World Bank, known formally as the International Bank for Reconstruction and Development, located in Washington, D.C., and loosely affiliated with both the United Nations and the International Monetary Fund, is the greatest institutional offender against common sense on the face of the Earth. Originally established to finance reconstruction in Europe after World War II and now oriented toward Third-World development, over the past twenty years the World Bank has compiled a record of human, environmental and economic disasters unmatched except in war and natural calamity. Controlled primarily by the G-7 wealthy industrialized nations, the United States having more than twice as many shares as any other member, the Bank has nonetheless been hotly denounced by many of the governments that, paradoxically, continue to fund it. Attacked by news organizations ranging from *60 Minutes* to the leftwing *Nation* to the rightwing *Economist,* and by scores of environmental groups, international health agencies, ex-officials, and in scathing internal reviews, the Bank has recently doubled its power.

It's just common sense that individuals and institutions must be in some way obliged to answer for their actions—governments to their constituents, companies to their stakeholders, each of us in our daily life. But so bizarrely secretive is this Bank, which now controls more than $150 billion in capital, much of it your tax money, that it is accountable to virtually no one. Not even the Bank's own directors, who make all major economic decisions, are allowed to see documents about Bank projects until two weeks before they vote yea or nay. Loopholes the size of the state of Florida have been buried in the fine print of legendarily voluminous reports. Mostly, directors depend on the arguments of the project leaders, and mostly, they agree with what they are told.

This byzantine cabal has gained the authority to operate secretly in any developing nation in the world. Once it has gained authority from top government officials, the Bank has no obligation to tell local residents or community leaders of its plans, even if the plans include massive destruction. This is a classic sweetheart arrangement, where the Bank and the national government excuse each other from being accountable to the people. It's as though they could obtain permission from Washington to build a dam and flood out your community without you or your mayor even having the right to know that it was going to happen.

This, in fact, is exactly what is happening with India's proposed Sardar Sarovar Dam, formally denounced but not derailed by the parliaments of the European Community, Japan, Finland and Sweden. Called "India's greatest planned environmental disaster," Sardar Sarovar was launched with neither the input nor the consent of the people who would be affected. In 1993, Sardar Sarovar sparked massive civil unrest over the prospect of creating several hundred thousand "development refugees," most of whom will not be humanely relocated. According to an investigation led by Barber Conable, former president of the World Bank, and prior to that, a conservative Republican congressman from New York, the Bank neglected to conduct fundamental environmental and human impact assessment studies when the project was begun a decade ago. Common sense says the World Bank knew that it didn't want to know.

Bottom line: the Bank is funded by wealthy nations to develop poor nations on terms favorable to the wealthy. Neither sinister nor noble, just business. "Let's face it: you can't have development without people getting hurt," said David Hopper, Bank senior vice president. Cynical, but a basic egg-omelette point. Particularly in overpopulated developing nations such as India, progress rarely comes without human suffering. The trouble with the World Bank, however, is that the suffering tends to come without the progress. By spearheading the infamous Polonoroeste project of the early 1980s, a vast road-building and agricultural colonization undertaking in the Rondônia area in northwest Brazil, a chunk of Amazon rainforest the size of Great Britain was torched, but to no good agricultural or economic effect: they decimated the forest and the culture and didn't net a dime! In a strategy executed under the pathetic direction of A. W. Clausen, the World Bank lent several hundred million dollars, attracting almost a billion more. Some of the finest tropical rainforest in the world was turned into desert. The landless poor who flocked by the hundreds of thousands to farm in Polonoroeste saw their topsoil disappear with the first rain.

The 1988 Christmastime murder of Chico Mendes, leader of the Brazilian rubber-tappers union who valiantly opposed the Polonoroeste project, has caused many to attribute dark motives to the World Bank. But one veteran bank hand quipped recently, "If the road to hell is paved with good intentions, then the World Bank will sooner or later build a six-lane superhighway, with subsidized buses and wheelchair access." Not evil, but idiocy of the highest intellectual caliber, is the charge. The World Bank is staffed by some of the most brilliant men (and they are mostly men) in the world, with top academic, diplomatic and corporate affiliations. In Polonoroeste, however, their collective wisdom somehow proved less than that of Smokey the Bear.

Then again, common sense says nothing ventured, nothing gained; anyone can make a mistake—that sort of thing, particularly deep in the jungle. When Conable took over from Clausen, he also took the high road, acknowledging that "the bank misread the human, institutional and physical realities of the jungle and the frontier," in Polonoroeste. Declaring that "If the World Bank has been part of the problem in the past, it can and will be a strong force in finding solutions in the future," Conable dramatically increased the Bank's environmental staff. Since the mid-1980s, the World Bank has hosted a number of fine environmental symposia, producing many reports of very high quality. Problem is, no one with any power pays them a second thought.

"[The Bank's] written assurances don't amount to a hill of beans; they don't exist for practical purposes. Where do the pressures come from, pressing down on the World Bank to degrade its own procedures and to bring its own integrity into question?" demanded congressman James Scheuer (D-NY) in a 1989 House subcommittee hearing on World Bank policies. The pressure comes from the Bank's having just too much money, according to Bruce Rich, an attorney for the Environmental Defense Fund and author of *Mortgaging the Earth: The*

World Bank, Environmental Impoverishment and the Crisis of Development (1993). "Bank staff advance their careers by building up large loan portfolios and keeping them moving, not by slowing down the project pipeline to ensure environmental and social quality," writes Rich. He adds that the situation has worsened considerably since 1988 when, after years of intense lobbying, the Bank received a massive capital increase of $75 billion, nearly doubling its lending capacity. The directors' winning argument: that the Third World is falling behind in its debt payments, and so more money must be lent for them to build up and pay everything back.

The only thing increasing faster than the Bank's need to lend money is the failure rate of the projects it funds. According to a 1992 internal review conducted by Bank vice president Willi Wappenhans, the Bank's failure rate has more than doubled, to almost 40 percent of its projects, as judged by its own criteria. Rich concludes that "meeting lending targets has taken precedence over the environmental, social and economic quality of projects."

Common sense says that any institution where decisions are made in obsessive secrecy, human and environmental considerations are ignored with impunity, and spectacular losses are rewarded by tens of billions in new public capital, is a threat to the general welfare. The World Bank is a menace.

Although there are other multilateral development banks, the World Bank is by far the most powerful and untouchable. That it has no real competition seems to be both a cause and an effect of its accelerating unaccountability. Lack of competition must also explain how the Bank recently managed to gain control of $20 billion set aside expressly for fostering sound environmental programs in developing nations. The upshot of the 1992 Earth Summit in Rio was to fund the Global

Environment Facility, coadministered by the UN's Environment and Development Programmes, and financially managed by . . . who else?

The World Bank is both a symbol and a symptom of the need for more common sense in running the world. For too long we have tacitly accepted the proposition that international politics and finance are too complex and arcane for ordinary, practical thinking; that the best thing is to leave it all to the experts. We know where "leaving it to the experts" in Washington, the state house or city hall can lead. Without the reality check, the simple common sense of the people for whose benefit the government is presumably being run, the experts would drive us to ruin, just as we amateurs would probably botch things without their expertise. Our participation is crucial to the sensible operation of individual societies. And so it should be in the global arena.

Back to the Common Future

"Common sense is recognizing that we have a common future together," said Gro Harlem Brundtland, prime minister of Norway, during a brief interview in New York. Brundtland, who strives to be Secretary General of the United Nations, regards the world with the same working familiarity with which most leaders regard their own nation. She is a quintessential one-worlder, convinced that the Earth is a closed system and that what happens anywhere affects everywhere, whether we notice it or not. Arguing that poverty in the Third World and overconsumption by the wealthiest nations are the greatest threats to the general welfare, it is therefore in the rich nations' best interest to help less-developed countries move as quickly as possible through the pollution phase of their evolution. "We cannot tell the developing countries that the wastebasket is full and leave it at that. Call that common sense if you like. They won't listen and the whole world will suffer."

As chairperson of the UN's World Commission on Environment and Development (UNCED), Brundtland tirelessly propounds the doctrine of sustainable development, which holds that economies should be based on renewable resources, such as sustained timber lands, rather than the one-time exploitation of natural preserves. The UNCED sponsored the 1992 Earth Summit in Rio de Janeiro, where the above-mentioned $20-billion global environment fund for developing nations was established. (The rationale for the World Bank's administering the fund was that otherwise a whole new bureaucracy would have been needed—that is, they had no alternative.) At the Rio summit, popularly known as Eco '92, phrases like "common future" and "sustainable development" became mantras of global cooperation. Of course we are all in this together. Of course we must all work for the common good.

But who, exactly, are "we"? Beyond basic genetic traits and fundamental emotions is there really a common human condition, or just an aggregate mass of humanity? Structuralist philosopher Jacques Derrida says common sense exists within a "domain of commitment," be that a local community, a society, or even an ethnic group, such as the world's Jewry, geographically farflung. Strolling through the crowds of Eco '92, the largest gathering of heads of state, nongovernmental representatives, and journalists in history, one got a magnificent sense of commitment to a global family, particularly because, unlike most diplomatic events, it seemed to have almost as many women participants as men. From almost all nations, faiths, and walks of life, 30,000 offspring had gathered to celebrate, and to defend, their Mother Earth.

Highs wear off, however, and the question of commitment remains. Does common sense really say that we Americans—or, for that matter, the peaceful, prosperous Norwegians whom Brundtland represents—should hasten to cast our lot with the underprivileged masses of the world? What's in it, common-sense-wise, for us?

One thinks of the world as divided into haves and have-nots, but according to Lester Brown of the Worldwatch Institute, about one billion people live in poverty, about one billion in luxury, and the rest, more than three billion, make up the middle class. In general, the world's middle class lives rather healthfully, by personal and ecological standards. They get most of their calories from grains and plant proteins, and less than 20 percent from fats, compared to the 30 percent figure for which Americans are assailed today. They use relatively little in the way of disposables, meaning that they don't pile up landfills with the plastics, cardboard, and foils that come with disposable diapers, microwavable-packaged frozen dinners, fast-food take-outs, and the like. They use most of their clothing until it wears out, or pass it on to someone else. The majority of the world's middle class drinks mostly fresh water, tea, coffee, and milk for the children; these beverages pose few environmental problems, for they are minimally packaged and consume little transport energy because they are moved only short distances or in dry form. The world's middle class rides bicycles (particularly in Asia), buses, and other forms of mass transportation, neither wasting much energy nor causing much pollution with automobiles or airplanes. Neither do they use much air conditioning or refrigeration, which not only waste energy but consume CFCs, adding to the greenhouse effect and damaging the ozone layer.

Sound familiar? The world's middle class lives a lot like our grandparents did. Back in the days when Waste not, want not wasn't some New Age ecological slogan, just thrifty good sense. When the idea of $3 for less than a pound of microwavable frozen french fries in their own use-once-and-throw-away oven-ready container would have seemed ridiculous, even if you had the bucks to burn. When hand-me-downs were a help, not a faux pas. Even if our grandparents didn't do much cycling, they could understand biking around town, spending nothing and getting a little exercise, better than paying to drive around in the car, then paying more to pump the Lifecycle at the health club because you're getting fat from all that driving around.

As common sense goes global, absorbing cultures and perspectives exotic to our own, in a fundamental way it also becomes more like what we've always known.

"We have found that if you put a collection tank on the rain gutters of a supermarket, you get enough water to irrigate the entire parking lot, even in the driest years. By coupling measures like these with planting trees, not only do you get a greener, cooler city better protected from a flood, but by cutting the runoff from the streets, you also get a much cleaner bay," says Andy Lipkis, forty, founder of the Treepeople organization in Los Angeles.

Catch the rainwater before it washes away. From time immemorial and from landscape to landscape, this is the kind of timeless, cultureless, simple good sense that has worked. Treepeople, a twenty-year-old environmental organization run by Lipkis, his wife Katie, and a small corps of staffers, has educated tens of thousands of schoolchildren with greencare projects and mobilized volunteers to plant millions of trees in greater Los Angeles. At its own initiative and on a shoestring budget,

Treepeople launched a four-year fruit-tree-planting project in six African nations, which ended with local citizens taking over their orchards and developing cottage industries with such products as dried fruits and jams. In 1987, UNCED singled out Treepeople among hundreds of competitors as the model United States voluntary organization for the environment.

Beyond the American Nose

We Americans have always been proud to share our ingenuity with the rest of the world. But learn from foreigners? The first step is to admit we have a problem with the whole idea. We have a peculiar perspective on the rest of the world—we are far better known than we are informed. Insulated by two oceans and the perfect neighbor to the north, a much greater proportion of American television and print journalism is devoted to domestic coverage than is typical anywhere else. Yet our daily doings are followed with soap-opera absorption by people around the globe.

Consider this curious fact: Never in the history of United States commercial broadcast television has a regularly scheduled entertainment series—comedy, drama or otherwise—been set outside the United States. Except for a few British offerings on public broadcasting channels and cable, no foreign series, or domestic series produced overseas, has ever made a dent on the television—ABC, NBC, CBS and FOX—that the average Nielsen householder watches for most of his or her twenty-eight plus viewing hours per week, a quarter of their waking time. On domestic television, characters may travel and adventure thither and yon but they are almost always American, living right here.

Outside the United States, the television diet is better balanced between domestic and international programming. Typically a range of shows come from the local culture, plus MTV,

CNN, BBC, plus a variety of foreign dramatic and adventure series, most of them American.

Quick, name a famous Chinese person alive today. Other than Deng Xiaoping. Now try the same for India, which together with China accounts for about 35 percent of the world's population. Add in Pakistan, Afghanistan, Bangladesh, the former USSR east of the Urals, southeast Asia, and the Koreas—that's around half the world's total, and still hardly anyone well known in the West. This blank even includes Japan, far better known for its society than its individuals. Save for the Dalai Lama, Ravi Shankar, the Maharishi Mahesh Yogi, Akira Kurosawa, that gigantic sumo wrestler, and the president of Sony, whose name is on the tip of your tongue, it is hard to think of any Asian person as familiar to the American public as Kermit the Frog. Yet Kermit, Mickey Mouse, Madonna, Michaels Jordan and Jackson, and so on may boast a billion Asian fans.

The handicaps to knowing less about potential partners or adversaries than they do about us are obvious. One sorry example is the United States prosthesis manufacturers who tried and failed to sell shoe-on artificial legs to the 900-million-person Indian market. They were either unaware or unwilling to accommodate to the reality that most Indians wear sandals or go barefoot.

The reverse side of ignorance is cultural arrogance, where we simply assume that our culture is the only game in town. Gary Wederspahn, a business consultant with the relocation firm of Moran, Stahl and Boyer International, tells of a U.S. Army general visiting Japan who opened a speech with a joke that had the punch line, "Show me, I'm from Missouri." The interpreter, knowing that his Japanese audience would have no idea what the American general meant, translated thus: "The general has made a joke and I'll be in trouble if you don't laugh." The audience obligingly burst into laughter, saving face for the interpreter, if not for the new world order.

At his Earth Summit press conference, Ted Turner filled his answers with obscure Americanisms, often assuming detailed knowledge about Atlanta, Las Vegas, and other United States locales. Journalists from Albania to Zimbabwe grew confused and upset at what sounded like the American's cultural condescension. How could this paragon of globalism, who has banned the word "foreign" from all CNN newscasts, possibly be so insensitive? It didn't take long for the journalists to turn, attacking Turner and all commercial television for promoting wasteful overconsumption, a big issue at the Earth Summit. Turner, who has probably done more high-quality environmental programming than all the other commercial networks combined, found himself unfairly scapegoated as a Yankee wastemonger.

We Americans have one great advantage over the rest of the world when it comes to knowing foreign languages and geography: low expectations. Well-to-do, confident, and friendly . . . Americans are expected to be. But culturally sophisticated—not. If Turner had made his references to Rio rather than Atlanta, or if the general had managed a punchline that everyone could get, the crowds would have been theirs. When John F. Kennedy declared at the Berlin Wall, "Ich bin ein Berliner!" the Germans rejoiced in his gracious gesture. That Kennedy had declared himself, idiomatically, to be a kind of local pastry, popularly known as a "Berliner," was smilingly excused—A for effort, heart in the right place, and all that. If Charles de Gaulle had made the same mistake, the German press would have been full of creampuff cartoons the next day.

Toward Multicultural CS

Eco '92 organizers showed some multicultural common sense in getting Roger Moore, internationally famous as a former "Agent 007," to be the official host. During the opening ceremonies on Flamingo Beach, excited crowds rushed the stage that was full of prime ministers, movie stars and other dignitaries. The structure swayed and threatened to collapse, yet no one would obey security's repeated orders to leave. Moore crisply commanded them back to their places with the reminder, "As you know, I can be very aggressive." And the multitudes obediently leaped back onto the sand. No matter their native language, everybody got the message that you don't mess with James Bond.

Multicultural common sense operates from the premise that human nature is the same everywhere. Like the way a handyman can go ahead and knock something together without instructions, the working assumption is that with a little common sense folks can build basic rapport. And that the rapport is worth building. Use whatever works to bridge cultural gaps.

Global common denominators are a good way to start. Once, I found myself in the company of three fellows from Soviet Georgia who did not speak a word of English, and I not a word of Russian or Georgian. The choice was to sit around uncomfortably or have a chat. One guy says, "Michael Jackson!" and up goes his thumb and those of his two comrades. Purely in the spirit of international cooperation, mine did too. My turn: "Prince!" three up, politely. From Whitney Houston and Julio Iglesias to Gorbachev, Reagan, Jesus, the names and their corresponding issues became more serious, and our thumbs ranged the full 180 degrees. The jury was hung on Josef Stalin, who, though hated and discredited, was still a Georgia boy.

We were doing what Richard Bandler and John Grinder, founders of the field of neuro-linguistic programming, would refer to as "reframing" the situation. Rather than mindlessly continuing on in a language unintelligible to the other, or worse, as often seems to happen when people of different tongues meet, repeating the same phrase over and over again, louder each time, an alternate mode of communication was established. Reframing, which means to reconsider a dilemma from a constructive perspective, can be as simple as, when language fails, asking for the time by tapping one's wrist. Or it can be as ambitious and creative as musicians from different parts of the world jamming and improvising to surmount their cultural barriers.

George Bush sagely remarked, "I remind myself a lot of this: We must conquer the temptation to assign bad motives to people who disagree with us." This is a fundamental principle of multicultural common sense, for the greater the differences, the likelier it is that disagreements will occur. Take the relationship between Western societies and fundamentalist Islamic cultures. More than common sense is needed to mend this rift. Yet imagine for a moment that some culture of superior wealth and force was bombarding our airwaves with sophisticated, alluring messages promoting drug use, homicidal carnage, and underage sex. Imagine how outraged we might feel as passive victims of this relentless, lurid propaganda, and to what lengths we might go to stop it. This is roughly how our popular culture looks to the Moslem world. From a Koranic perspective, J.R. and Sue Ellen downing scotches in front of their son is just a technicality away from snorting cocaine in the family bosom. Not to say that they don't get drunk and carry on in Islamic societies, just that it's not what they want projected into their homes, validated by images of glamour and wealth. The same "family-values" objections have been raised in this country, and the nighttime sin-soaps are on their way out, for the time being.

Multicultural common sense can work right around the corner. The same Malaysian woman seemed to be working every time I went to a neighborhood fruit and flower store, and so I asked her when she got her vacation. She said she doesn't have any vacation. "But everybody's got a vacation!" I exclaimed, causing the normally polite woman to double over in laughter. It was like I was some poor little rich boy who thought everybody had a Rolls-Royce. Quickly she translated for two co-workers, who dropped their nectarines. Competition from the Asian Rim could get pretty rough.

Let's say you have lunch at the same sandwich shop a couple of times a week, and that you like tomatoes on your sub but they charge extra for a few puny slices. The guy behind the counter, Ziad, is obviously not a native English speaker, and so you find out where he's from. Pakistan. Family here or there? Wife's here; she's from Pakistan too, but most of the family's back there. Child on the way. Congratulations! which you try to time for when he's reaching for the tomatoes.

Now Pakistan is a little bulb in your mind, and news about it takes on a new light. Like the story of Benazir Ali Bhutto, that beautiful woman, a Harvard graduate, who was removed from her nation's presidency. Next trip to the sub shop, Ziad tells how Benazir's father was also president and was executed by pretty much the same bunch who chased his daughter out of office. Ziad has a theory connecting her overthrow with the top-secret 1991 nuclear showdown between Pakistan and India, recently revealed in the news, that blind sheik allegedly connected to the World Trade Center bombing, and also that strange attack early in 1993 by a Pakistani national on CIA headquarters in Virginia. All of which is worth an extra pickle, at least.

When children of different cultural backgrounds play together, common sense lessons are inevitable. My friend Raul
Garcia of Miami was raised in a traditional Cuban culture,
where the custom was that if a guest openly admired a possession, then it was to be offered as a gift. From childhood, Raul
was taught a kind of hands-off appreciation for other people's
things, and expected such reserve in return. Raul had just gotten
a brand-new red fire truck for his birthday, and an Anglo friend
who had come over to play openly admired it, enthusiastically.
Raul had no choice but to hand the truck over. Raul went crying
to his mother, who taught him how to bridge the cultural gap
and get his truck back. She told him to take a ball and play with
it loudly, making like he was having a wonderful time and that
this was the best ball in the world. He did, and soon his little
friend came padding over to see what all the fun was, and you
know the rest of the story.

Sadly, it often takes the equivalent of global understanding just to bridge the cultural gaps between black and white
Americans. I, for one, had no idea that Michael Milken was
thought of as "Brother Milken" by many prominent African-
Americans, because a number of the companies he leveraged
with junk bonds were black-owned enterprises. According to
the *Amsterdam News,* a New York newsweekly, many members
of the black business community considered Milken's prosecu-
tion and imprisonment punishment for his politics. Far-fetched
from a mainstream perspective, but sensible to a community
that feels it has been systematically persecuted and demoralized.

Multicultural common sense is neither politically correct nor
incorrect: its standard is not justice but effectiveness. Jeff Shesol,
creator of the widely syndicated cartoon series *PC Person,* says
"Political correctness has been called intolerance of intolerance

but I think it's really intolerance of any other point of view." The 1991 Rhodes Scholar and self-described liberal derides "the cult of blamelessness," in which people care more about "their own ethical résumé" than getting things accomplished.

"I think you have to pick your fights," says Shesol. He explains that among today's students, the concept of right and wrong is one of words and images, rather than the palpable 1960s realities of the civil-rights movement, the Vietnam war, and so on, on which their parents were raised. They become as impassioned about fights over symbols as about fights over events, and sometimes the relative importance of words and action can become confused. Exemplifying PC confusion, he cites the policy that prevented the Brown University newspaper from printing that the suspect in a series of rapes and assaults around campus was a black male.

Out of the Cocoon

I explained in the Introduction the thesis of this book: that the worlds out there and in here are merging uncontrollably, creating confusion and challenging traditional common-sense notions. According to Faith Popcorn, CEO of BrainReserve, a New York City trend-analysis firm, the commonest American response has been to take refuge in the home. Popcorn is best known for coining the term "cocooning," defined as "the impulse to go *inside* just when it gets too tough and scary *outside*. To pull a shell of safety around yourself . . . a sort of hyper-nesting." Virtually anything that saves a foray into the dangerous world beyond is considered "on-trend." Called "the Nostradamus of marketing" by *Fortune* magazine, Popcorn predicts that more and more of our work, entertainment, shopping and even (simulated) travel will be done at home, via computer- and video-generated images and sensations. Cyberpunk gone mainstream is the essence of her vision.

There's a logic to cocooning—it expands the world in here while keeping external forces more or less at bay. Yet it fosters the illusion that the world out there can be controlled from one's personal headquarters, as though the two worlds are somehow coequivalent entities. In spirit, this reliance on high-tech security, minimized personal contact, and electronically mediated interaction is the opposite of the open-home tradition whereby guests are welcomed, new ideas are entertained, and mutual problems are solved. Popcorn claims that cocooning is part of a Save Our Society trend toward greater social consciousness, but fear, not the spirit of salvation, is why people hide out.

If the introduction of capital punishment resulted in a 99 percent decrease in homicides and other capital crimes, would you support it? How about a 10 percent decrease? 0.1 percent? No change? An increase?

If ever there were an issue where common sense got snarled in the introverted logic of the cocoon, it's the death penalty. From bleeding-heart handwringers to vicarious executioners who would zap the baddies with their TV remote controls, capital punishment has taken on an emotional reality far beyond its objective importance. By arguing about whether or not to kill the criminals, people seem to feel that they are *doing* something about crime and injustice. Campaigning Clinton had to be present for an execution in Arkansas to assure right-leaning skeptics that he was man enough for the kill. And New York Governor Mario Cuomo stands piously against the possibility of his state ever inflicting a wrongful death, while fifth-generation welfare gangs run riot through government housing.

The issue becomes not how secure people actually are but how safe they feel in their nests. Meanwhile the more substantive but less telegenic issues of swifter justice and humane rehabilitation get short shrift. These are less relevant to the cocoon's convoluted emotional realities.

Hypernesters tend to incubate irrational anxieties. I have a friend, a sharp, reliable professional woman who, over the years, has become ever more fearful of venturing beyond her home and her daily routine. If a terrorist bomb goes off on an international flight, for the next year she will refuse to fly, even though the Caribbean is her favorite for vacations. Same response with earthquakes, which have thus far prevented her from visiting California, a state she probably would enjoy. It's not a case of innumeracy. This person is highly educated and fully understands that the odds of having an auto accident, getting mugged or robbed, and other risks are exponentially higher than suffering some statistical freak of an accident. But the further she withdraws from workaday reality, the more certain she becomes that the one-in-a-zillionth chance has her name on it.

We are fortunate, thus far, that no one has figured out how to commit murder over the telephone. Suicide, at least of the financial variety, is not only possible but increasingly common via telecommunications. One may pick up the phone and in a few hours spend hundreds of dollars on chat and sex-talk lines; recorded messages from rock groups, real-estate companies and fortune tellers; interactive quiz games and lotteries; and of course credit-card shopping. Next up, according to Popcorn, is the "1000" number, sort of an upscale 900, through which consumers will be able to hold forth with mechanics, financial planners, psychiatrists, lawyers and sundry other experts at minute-by-minute fees. For most of us the telephone presents no more of a threat than, say, the general availability of sedatives. Yet for persons who are unemployed, depressed, vulnerable, or desperate, dialing 1-900-HOW DUMB is at least a form of contact. The television set just doesn't respond—yet.

Cocoons are made to be broken.

However understandable, the impulse to hide from the outside world can be every bit as senseless as a butterfly trying to crawl back into its silk pouch. The disconcerting truth is that common sense doesn't necessarily come from doing what feels most comfortable. Starting with Frederick Herzberg's groundbreaking studies in the 1950s, management psychologists have consistently found that workers' performance on the job correlates less closely with high levels of satisfaction than with a moderate degree of stress and unease. Certainly the recent experience of the United States labor force, with jobs and benefits cut, pressure and hours increased, and productivity pumped up, bears out this unfortunate fact.

The same CS deficit may even hold true for the comforts of home. A 1990 psychological study at the New Orleans Veterans Medical Center showed that thirty homeless veterans with chronic mental illness had more common sense than thirty mentally ill counterparts who had been securely housed in the community. After administering a battery of intelligence, personality and coordination tests, Edward F. Foulks, William G. McCown, Melanie Duckworth, and Patricia B. Sutker of the Medical Center's psychiatry service found that the homeless subjects were relatively superior on measures of cognitive efficiency, problem solving, common-sense reasoning, and observation of detail. The reason, in a nutshell, is that the homeless men had to stay sharp and fend for themselves.

Back Across the Bridge

Garnet, a man in my neighborhood who makes his living selling discarded books and record albums on the street, had his right arm broken recently by another homeless man who tried to steal his shopping cart. A few weeks later, the great blizzard of 1993 hit. Aside from making things uncomfortable for those who spend their time outdoors, it meant that good money could be made by shoveling snow. But Garnet's arm was in a cast. What to do? He went to a local hardware store where they don't chase him away and begged and borrowed a bag of rock salt. (He insisted on putting up his entire sales inventory, ostensibly as good-faith collateral but actually just to have a safe place to leave the stuff.) Carrying the bag in the crook of his cast arm, he sold his services as a salt spreader, and let the other guys do the heavy work.

For a nice secure home, Garnet would trade his street savvy in a second. If the price is losing a few CS points, Garnet's common sense says Pay. More than at any time since World War II, great waves of refugees are on the move, sweeping north from Africa and Latin America, and west from Asia and the former Soviet empire. And though they may not know a word of English, or ever set foot on our continent, most of them understand Garnet's life better than you or I ever will. For them it's exactly the same—make do, or die. And wish they didn't have to.

Conclusion:
But Is It CS?

Not long after Richard Nixon's celebrated trip to China, two African-American jazz musicians were invited to teach at a Beijing university. On the first day of class, they asked to hear a tune, any tune at all, so one of the assisting professors strode to the piano and dutifully performed "The East Is Red." Then the jazzmen took over. The pianist stepped up the tempo, slipped in some scales, vamped a few chords. The sax, a punster, played phrases backwards and forwards, squeaking and honk ing in ways that, even allowing for cultural differences, didn't sound entirely respectful to Chairman Mao. Talk about a cultural revolution. East met West and turned red, white, blue, black and green.

The Chinese students reacted much the way that American audiences did to José Feliciano's legendary from-the-gut *Star Spangled Banner*—they were either thrilled or appalled. So it is with common sense today. The old familiar tune is being played a thousand different ways and we've got to get used to it. But how do you tell, in this multi-cultural-modal-dimensional age, the real CS article?

My hope is that the question, "But is it CS?", will become a general standard of judgment, à la PC for "politically correct," though without the ideological slant. Duke Ellington's rule was, "If it sounds good, it is good." But when it comes to common sense you can't just sing scat, no matter how clever it sounds. The following rules are intended as a guide to what's CS and what isn't, regardless of the rendition.

1. Common sense always rings true.

Plausibility, Raymond Chandler observed, is largely a matter of style. The CS-style is deft and often sharpened by wit, though not just for the sake of wordplay or to the point of being dismissed as a joke: the West African proverb, "No one tests the depth of the river with both feet," hits the tone in any language.

For all their air of authority, CS maxims and proverbs are anything but consistent from one to the next. They remind us that he who hesitates is lost, though haste does make waste, except while seizing the moment. More important than being logically unexceptionable is that a saying is handy in a pinch. "Look before you leap" is a compact phrase, easy to recall as one comes up to the edge. The same advice, phrased something like "be sure to examine all that lies beyond before impetuously venturing forward," would prevent fewer concussions.

The same rules apply for new CS sayings: "Every time you hate you taste the poison first." From nicotine to heroin, it has long been common knowledge that poisons are addictive and deadly. This new maxim from the Silva meditation program adds to the list whatever the neurococktail that's brewed by a festering mind.

2. It may not mean a thing even if it has that CS swing.

What rings CS true can nonetheless be outmoded or false. "If God had intended us to fly, we'd have been born with wings," has the tone but not the substance. So does "A woman's place is in the kitchen."

In *All I Really Need to Know I Learned in Kindergarten* (1986), Robert Fulghum offers this bit of pseudosagacity: "Anything not worth doing is worth not doing well. Think about it." (This was written on a note from a cobbler who, unable to fix Fulghum's shoes, inserted chocolate-chip cookies in them instead.) Without the "nots," this sentiment is indeed a valued maxim, but if you really "think about it," the opposite of wisdom is rarely worthwhile.

Like any other style, CS can be mimicked for ulterior purposes. Marketers have a powerful stake in convincing us that buying their goods is the common-sense thing to do. Kellogg's Common Sense Oat Bran; Sears's Discover card, called "A refresher course in common sense," are among the latest attempts. More artful than simply plastering on the label are those who mimic the CS-style: "You never have a second chance to make a first impression," goes the tag line from an advertisement for Head and Shoulders shampoo; "Nobody cares less about your ego than a stopwatch," warns a Speedo swimsuit ad. "Motorists wise, Simonize!" made it a smart thing to go out and wax the car.

3. Beware of BS in CS form.

"Being smart has nothing to do with being nice," says novelist Laurence Shames, who delights in exposing the illusions of depth, morality, and significance that sustain contemporary egos. From Shames's perspective, wishful thinkers who fuzzily equate common sense and common decency or otherwise sanctify simple human savvy do a disservice. By falling into the habit of assuming that those who are intelligent are also good, we are ripe for the plucking by the smart ones who aren't.

Some people are just better at seeming than being. When EST guru Werner Erhard raked in contributions from the throng of devotees who jammed Madison Square Garden to support his "Hunger Project," he drew wild applause by announcing that not one penny would go to feed hungry people! No, this money would go to talking about the problem of hunger, about how, when, where, why, and to what degree people were hungry. And to raising more money for Erhard to talk about it all even more.

Let them eat words?

"Of all the dumb ways to save money, not feeding babies is the dumbest," was a favorite saying of Dr. Jean Mayer, a crusading nutritionist who relentlessly buttonholed politicians with that argument. Mayer understood that talking about a problem is only one step toward solving it. The former president of Tufts University, decorated by Charles de Gaulle for heroism during World War II, personally persuaded President Richard Nixon to create the food-stamp program in 1969. And Mayer followed up from then on, helping to design and sponsor subsequent antihunger programs providing nutritional assistance to pregnant women and infant children.

4. The CS instinct is to get the job done.

"Common sense is making your best guess and going with it," says British scientist James Lovelock, best known for his Gaia theory of global ecology. Lovelock points out that some of the most important public-policy decisions have been made on common sense and instinct; science usually comes after the fact. He gives the example of how public-health officials arrested the first cholera epidemics by investigating the areas hardest hit by the plague. They saw that human waste was leaking into the water supply and, rather than waiting for scientific verification of their suspicions, decided to clean up the contamination.

In *Healing Gaia: Practical Medicine for the Planet* (1991), Lovelock writes "No one doubts that CFCs [chlorofluoro-carbon aerosols] have reached a level that is already damaging. . . . Sensible greens are puzzled about why, if this is so, we continue to spend billions of scarce funds on stratospheric and ozone depletion research, when the problem is in effect solved. We know the poison, all that needs doing is to stop imbibing it." Lovelock, the scientist who originally discovered CFCs in the atmosphere but argued against banning them because their concentrations were so low, now argues quite sensibly that it's time to clean up. Time to get on with the low-tech, low-glamour hard work of going out into the world and patching up leaking air conditioners, removing freon from discarded refrigerators and the like.

Moscow writer Fazil Iskander describes a society where the connection between work and reward has been lost. "Everything or nothing—this is the philosophy of a people subconsciously believing they are unable or unwilling to do anything. When all we have to do is stand up, get a bucket of water and water our pumpkins, we prefer discussing ways of saving mankind. The more our pumpkins need watering, the more high-flown our discussions of salvation become," he said in an interview with *The New York Times*.

Sometimes common sense goes right out the window. Former astronaut James Lovell, who recalls being able to put his thumb up to the window and completely block out the Earth,

tells the story of the ill-fated Apollo 13 mission, which suffered
an explosion in the lunar module. Lovell tried frantically to
explain the extreme seriousness of the situation to the two
junior astronauts under his command—they were going to be
stranded on the Moon! But his cohorts could not or would not
react and instead kept looking out the window and taking pictures of the scenery. Lovell finally got through with the
reminder that if they didn't deal with the emergency pronto,
their photos would never be developed.

To Henning Dyremose, Denmark's Minister of Finance, it
was perfectly obvious that Danish voters would ratify the
Maastricht agreement on European economic unification, because Denmark would thereby become the linchpin for trade between Western Europe and the rest of Scandinavia. So confident
were Dyremose and his fellow government officials that they
made little effort to campaign for the fait accompli. But early in
1992 the voters narrowly rejected Maastricht, setting in motion
a wave of misgivings and exceptions that imperiled the agreement throughout the European Community. A year later Danish voters did approve a weakened version of the treaty, though
without committing to a common European currency or defense.

"Common sense is whatever the voters say it is," Dyremose
now repeats and repeats.

5. *Common sense is a good projective test.*

"As a wiseguy, you can lie, you can cheat, you can steal, you
can kill people—legitimately! You can do any goddamn thing
you want, and nobody can say anything about it. Who *wouldn't*
want to be a wiseguy?" said Lefty Ruggiero, a former associate
of the Bonanno organized crime family. Macabre as it seems,
Ruggiero not only treasures his supposed license to commit
mayhem, he takes for granted that's what you live for, too.

What someone considers "just common sense" may be valuable and telling, even if it makes no sense at all. "Common sense? I've got one. Don't sleep with your boss unless you're sure to get the promotion," said an ex-employee of the ace New York real-estate developer. Within her code, perfectly shrewd.

Most people's opinions about common sense are as emphatic and direct as the subject itself, but sometimes a little decoding is necessary: "Never allow yourself to be stressed when you are fully extended," replies Doug Brignole, who has held the titles of Mr. Universe, Mr. America and Mr. California. The statement that has the feel of a CS rule for survival in these frenetic times started out as a fitness tip against the danger of bench presses.

Other responses preclude all debate. "Listen. Common sense ain't got nothing to do with boxing," says former middleweight champion Jake LaMotta, with a growl. Now, one could argue that under Olympic rules boxing is more like fencing, with the number of blows landed deemed more important than the amount of damage inflicted, and that this rule lends a significant measure of sanity to the sport. But one wouldn't.

6. Couples have their own form of common sense.

"Who's got more Common Sense? I do. No, Curtis does, because he's a husband who defers to his wife," says Lisa Sliwa, cofounder of the Guardian Angels urban patrol organization, before her husband gets out a word. Curtis, who since took six bullets and still had wits enough to save himself by diving out a taxicab window, does a good-natured slow burn. He dutifully reminds me that his wife has written a book and stars in a home video, both entitled *Common Sense Self-Defense*.

What's CS to couples when they are together may be quite different than what it is to either member alone. And whether or not they agree is often less telling than the way they go about it.

"Common sense? Well, that means dealing with nonsense at least half the time," said Judith Karolyi, a Hungarian noblewoman who has spent much of her life running an artistic foundation in southern France. Her life companion, Zenka Bartek, a British literary reviewer, takes exception: "I should say more often than that."

7. Powerful people can define what's CS.

Consider Warren Buffett, known as the "Sage of Omaha" for having made his $5-billion-plus personal fortune by shrewd investing. Credited with saving the Salomon Inc. Wall Street investment house from scandalous collapse, Buffett has the CS style: modest in lifestyle, moderate in politics, stressing that the whole point of investing is to take the least risk necessary, not the most. Not one for computers or calculators, America's second-richest man, according to *Forbes,* manages Berkshire Hathaway corporation's $18 billion in assets mostly in his head, and writes his annual reports with homespun wisdom and wit.

"I recall that one woman, upon being asked to describe the perfect spouse, specified an archeologist: 'The older I get,' she said, 'the more interested he'll be in me.' She would have liked my tastes: I treasure those extraordinary Berkshire managers who are working well past normal retirement age, and who concomitantly are achieving results much superior to those of their younger competitors. . . . It's hard to teach a new dog old tricks," writes Buffett in the Berkshire Hathaway annual report for 1992.

To Buffett, it's just obvious that in stock-shopping, like anything else, one hunts for the best bargains. He believes that the worst time to buy a stock is when the price is going up. That other, equally impressive fortunes have been made by investing when a stock starts its upward run is a quibble. Unless of course, the argument were made by, for example, Bernard Baruch, the legendary financier who made his fortune by jumping in early and "selling too soon." Then common sense would say, agree with him too.

"A radical is a man with both feet planted firmly in the air," quipped Franklin Roosevelt, a true common-sense arbiter. In addition to inherent good judgment, what gives certain individuals the power to define common sense is, just that, power. Although we don't necessarily associate common sense with the ruling elite, and might argue strenuously that's exactly what they lack, the centrist orientation of compromise, conservativism, and attention to pragmatics rather than (infectious) ideology, is ultimately in the interest of those who control the status quo. C. Edwin Baker, professor of constitutional law at the University of Pennsylvania, observes, "All too frequently, common sense is a way the majority imposes its prejudice. It codifies the biases of the dominant ideology."

8. What's common sense, all too often, is what's common sense to men.

Over the past decade I have written on topics in hard science, finance and other traditionally male-dominated subjects, and never have I seen such an imbalance as the outlandish extent to which male thinkers have controlled scholarship and general commentary on the subject of common sense. Presumably women's accelerating accession to socioeconomic power will eventually redress this arrangement, but as it stands, the published insights and pronouncements that shape common-sense thinking run dozens to one in favor of the men.

If for no other reason than their comparative restraint from irrational violence, women just seem more CS than men.

Wangari Mathaii, leader of the Kenyan Greenbelt ecological democracy movement which, staffed and directed mostly by women, has motivated millions throughout Africa, was recently beaten unconscious by government police and left for dead. She recovered, however, and at the 1992 Earth Summit in Rio explained that one type of supposed common sense—keeping your mouth shut for fear of reprisal—is something that women in her country are learning to ignore. "As long as we meet to plant trees, the men are fine, the government is fine. But as soon as we ask about who owns the land we are planting, and why that is, then they tell us we are out of our minds."

Judge Mary Leikes, who recently became the first woman to serve on the District Court of Nebraska, believes that common sense is something that women just naturally have more of: "Oh golly, I see it in my courtroom all the time. The women attorneys know when to stop, and when to shut their clients up. The men, bless them, just keep going on and on," says Leikes.

Although the legal embodiment of the concept of common sense, known as ORP Man (ordinary, reasonable, prudential man), has evolved to become ORP person, Leikes sees the transition as mostly semantic, except in specific areas such as sexual harassment, where it now must encompass what a woman might find offensive. "The basic concept of common sense hasn't changed, and I don't see why it should," says Leikes, explaining that sensible behavior, such as driving as a reasonable person might drive, is not a matter of gender.

One observation: Both Mathaii and Leikes declined to define common sense, considering themselves unqualified. Unlike these highly accomplished women, no man interviewed for this book found himself similarly unsuited.

9. *Common sense is humble at heart.*

Abraham Lincoln had a riddle: How many legs does a dog have if you call his tail a leg? The answer: four. A tail isn't a leg just because you say so.

"Common sense is knowing what you can do and knowing what you can't do, and not letting your ego tell you any different. Lots of guys get to the big leagues and it goes right to their head," said baseball pitching star Tommy John. The way to keep from blowing it all, says John who, when he retired, was the oldest player in the major leagues, is "By remembering where you come from, which, in my case, is Terre Haute, Indiana."

Down-home wisdom fits like an old pair of blue jeans. "Horse sense is what keeps horses from betting on what people do," is how Raymond Nash defines it. "Don't ever buy anything that eats," advises Texas pundit Joe Bob Briggs. And after reading aloud an ad for a local shoestore, Early Wright, host of a daily blues radio program in Clarksdale, Mississippi, adds "Buy your shoes big enough so as not to cause your toes any ailment. If your toenails aren't growing, then your shoes aren't big enough."

10. *Using common sense is doing the right thing.*

Common sense is the workaday wisdom one is expected to have. It's the craft of reasonable living, not the art of pondering Life. We have the right to demand it, and the obligation to use it because no matter how much individual interpretations may differ, everyone agrees that common sense helps make the world a little saner.

Bibliography

Aach, John. "Science and Commonsense Skepticism." *The Skeptical Inquirer* (Fall 1991).

Applebaum, R. A. *U.S. Department of Transportation Navigation Rules: International and Inland*. Washington, D.C.: U.S. Printing Office, 1990.

Applewhite, Ashton, William R. Evans III, and Andrew Frothingham, eds. *And I Quote: The Definitive Collection of Quotes, Sayings, and Jokes for the Contemporary Speaker*. New York: St. Martin's Press/Thomas Dunne, 1991.

Ariès, Philippe, and George Duby, gen. eds. *A History of Private Life: Vol. I—From Pagan Rome to Byzantium*. Cambridge: Belknap/ Harvard University Press, 1987.

Associated Press report. "County Writes 136-Word Definition for Buttocks." Key West: *Key West Citizen,* March 19, 1992.

Baker, C. Edwin. "The Ideology of the Economic Analysis of Law." *Philosophy & Public Affairs* (Fall 1975).

Bandler, Richard and John Grinder. *Reframing: Neuro-Linguistic Programming and the Transformation of Meaning*. Moab, Utah: Real People Press, 1982.

Bark, William Carroll. *Origins of the Medieval World.* Stanford, Calif.: Stanford University Press, 1958.

Bartlett, John; Emily Morison Beck, ed. *Familiar Quotations.* Boston: Little, Brown, 1968.

Benedict, Ruth. *The Chrysanthemum and the Rose.* Boston: Houghton Mifflin, 1946.

Bleil, Bryan. "The Brain Trust." *Texas Monthly* (October 1990).

Bolen, Jean Shinoda. *Goddesses in Everywoman.* San Francisco: Harper & Row, 1984.

Boswell, James. *The Life of Samuel Johnson.* London: Penguin Books, 1986.

Bower, Bruce. "Consciousness Raising: Theories Abound Regarding the Vexing Nature of Conscious Experience." *Science News* (October 10, 1992).

———. "Rethinking the Mind: Cognitive Science Faces a Philosophical Challenge." *Science News* (October 17, 1992).

Broder, Tanya. "Alabama Woman Eaten by Plant from Outer Space!" *Weekly World News* (November 24, 1992).

Bronowski, J. *The Common Sense of Science.* Cambridge: Harvard University Press, 1978.

Brown, Lester R. *State of the World 1991: A Worldwatch Institute Report on Progress Toward a Sustainable Society.* New York: W. W. Norton, 1991.

Buffett, Warren E. "Chairman's Letter." *Berkshire Hathaway Inc.: 1992 Annual Report.* Omaha, Neb.: 1993.

Clark, Kelly James. "Spanish Common Sense Philosophy: Jaime Balmes' Critique of Cartesian Foundationalism." *History of Philosophy Quarterly* (April 1990).

Collins, James. "What Could We Have Been Thinking?" *Spy* (April 1991).

Coursey, David. "Scientist Finds Common Sense for Computing in Gossip Tabloid." *MIS Week* (March 19, 1990).

Davis, L. J. "Buffett Takes Stock." *The New York Times Magazine* (April 1, 1990).

Dennett, Daniel C. *Consciousness Explained.* Boston: Little, Brown, 1991.

Dowling, John C. "Opinion: The Tale of the Dispossessed Doctor, or, Mistress Molly and Her Lover's Folly," Gary Lewis, plaintiff vs. Molly E. Bartlett, defendant, Case no. 3578-S-1989. Court of Common Pleas, Dauphin County, Pennsylvania, July 1991.

Dracup, Chris, in "News and Notes," *RSS News.* London: Royal Statistical Society (May 1991).

Einstein, Albert. "Physics and Reality." Orig. Pub. 1936, in *Essays in Physics.* New York: Philosophical Library, 1950.

Elvin, Herbert Lionel. *The Place of Commonsense in Educational Thought.* London: G. Allen & Unwin, 1977.

Emerson, Ralph Waldo. "Heroism," in *Essays: First and Second Series.* Orig. Pub. 1841. New York: Vintage Books, 1990.

Fletcher, Garth J. O. "Psychology and Common Sense." *American Psychologist* (March 1984).

Forguson, Lynd. *Common Sense.* New York: Routledge, 1989.

Foulks, Edward F., William G. McCown, Melanie Duckworth, and Patricia B. Sutker. "Neuropsychological Testing of Homeless Mentally Ill Veterans." *Hospital and Community Psychiatry* (June 1990).

Franklin, Benjamin, writing as "Richard Saunders." *Poor Richard's Almanack.* Orig. Pub. 1732–1757. New York: Paddington, 1976.

Freedman, David H. "Common Sense and the Computer." *Discover* (August 1990).

Fulghum, Robert. *All I Really Need to Know I Learned in Kindergarten: Uncommon Thoughts on Common Things.* New York: Ivy Books/ Ballantine, 1986.

Gardner, Howard. *Frames of Mind: The Theory of Multiple Intelligences.* New York: BasicBooks/Harper Collins, 1985.

Geertz, Clifford. "Common Sense as a Cultural System," *Antioch Review* (Spring 1975).

Grave, S. A. "Common Sense," in *The Encyclopedia of Philosophy: Vol. 2.* Paul Edwards, ed. in chief. New York: MacMillan/Free Press, 1967.

Guha, R. V. *Contexts: A Formalization and Some Applications.* Doctoral diss., Computer Science Dept. Stanford University and technical report ACT-CYC-342-91, Microelectronics and Computer Technology Corp., December 1991.

Guha, R. V., and Douglas B. Lenat. "Cyc: a Mid-Term Report," *AI Magazine* (Fall 1990).

Hale, Judson, ed. *The Best of the Old Farmer's Almanac: The First 200 Years.* New York: Random House, 1991.

Hegel, G. W. F. *The Phenomenology of Mind.* Orig. Pub. 1807. New York: Harper Torchbooks, 1967.

Holmes, Oliver Wendell. *The Poet at the Breakfast Table: He Talks to His Fellow-Boarders and the Reader.* Orig. Pub. 1872. Grosse Pointe, Mich.: Scholarly Press, 1968.

Johnson, Samuel. *A Dictionary of the English Language: in Which the Words Are Deduced from Their Originals, and Illustrated in Their Different Significations by Examples from the Best Writers, to Which Are Prefixed, a History of the Language, and an English Grammar.* Orig. Pub. 1755. New York: AMS Press, 1967.

Jonasson, Bjorn. *Havamal: The Sayings of the Vikings.* Reykjavik, Iceland: Gudthrun, 1992.

Joseph, Lawrence E. "Is Science Common Sense," in *Mysteries of Life and the Universe: New Essays from America's Finest Writers on Science.* William H. Shore, ed. New York: Harcourt Brace Jovanovich, 1992.

Kahn, Herman. *World Economic Development: 1979 and Beyond.* Boulder, Colo.: Westview Press, 1979.

Kant, Immanuel. "On the Supposed Right to Lie from Benevolent Motives." Orig. Pub. 1797, in *Critique of Practical Reason, and Other Writings in Moral Philosophy,* Lewis White Beck, ed. New York: Garland, 1976.

Keeshan, Bob. *Growing Up Happy: Captain Kangaroo Tells Yesterday's Children How to Nurture Their Own*. New York: Doubleday/Bantam/Dell, 1989.

Kilborn, Peter T. "From Homemaker to Wage Earner in Appalachia." *The New York Times* (July 7, 1991).

Kimball, Roger. *Tenured Radicals: How Politics Has Corrupted Our Higher Education*. New York: HarperPerennial/HarperCollins, 1991.

Kirk, Russell. *The Conservative Mind: From Burke to Eliot*. Lake Shore, Ill.: Regnery Books, 1986.

Koestler, Arthur. *The Roots of Coincidence*. New York: Vintage Books/Random House, 1973.

Kolata, Gina. "Brains at Work." *The New York Times* (January 6, 1991).

Kristol, Irving. "What Ever Happened to Common Sense?" *Reader's Digest* (February 1990).

Kuflik, Arthur. "A Defense of Common-Sense Morality." *Ethics* (July 1986).

Langer, Ellen J. *Mindfulness*. Reading, Mass.: Addison-Wesley/Merloyd Lawrence, 1989.

Lenat, D. B. and R. V. Guha. "Ideas for Applying Cyc," technical report ACT-CYC-407-91, December, 1991.

Levey, Judith S., and Agnes Greenhall, eds. *The Concise Columbia Encyclopedia*. New York: Columbia University Press, 1983.

Liu, Alan. "Toward a Theory of Common Sense: Beckford's Vathek and Johnson's Rasselas." *Texas Studies in Literature and Language* (Summer 1984).

Locke, John. *Two Treatises of Civil Government*. Orig. Pub. 1690. London: Dent, 1924.

Lopez-Pintor, Rafael. "The Role of Values in Social Research and Their Aid to Centers of Decision." *Revista Española de la Opinión Pública* (Madrid: October, 1973).

Lovelock, James. *Healing Gaia: Practical Medicine for the Planet*. London: Gaia Books; New York: Harmony Books/Crown, 1991.

Mackay, Charles. *Extraordinary Popular Delusions and the Madness of Crowds*. New York: Bonanza Books/Crown, 1981.

Magnusson, Sigurdur A. *The Icelanders*. Reykjavik, Iceland: Forskot, 1990.

Matthews, Jay. *Escalante: The Best Teacher in America*. New York: Holt, 1988.

Minsky, Marvin. *The Society of Mind*. New York: Simon & Schuster, 1986.

Mulvaugh, Jane. "Dictators by Design." London: *The European* (July 12, 1991).

Murphy, John W. "Jacques Derrida: A Rhetoric that Deconstructs Common Sense." *Diogenes* (Winter 1984).

Nathan, George Jean. *Autobiography of an Attitude*. New York: Knopf, 1925.

Nitecki, Joseph Z. "In Search of Sense in Common Sense Management." *Journal of Business Ethics*. Vol. 6 (1987).

Norman, Donald A. *The Design of Everyday Things*. New York: Doubleday/Bantam/Dell, 1989.

Oakes, Jeannie. *Keeping Track: How Schools Structure Inequality*. New Haven: Yale University Press, 1985.

Orwell, George. *1984*. Orig. Pub. 1949. New York: Harcourt Brace Jovanovich, 1977.

Paine, Thomas. *Common Sense*. Orig. Pub. 1776. Harmondsworth, Middlesex, Eng.: Penguin Books, 1976.

Parfit, Derek. *Reasons and Persons*. Oxfordshire: Oxford University Press, 1984.

Paulos, John Allen. *Innumeracy: Mathematical Illiteracy and its Consequences*. New York: Hill and Wang/Farrar, Straus & Giroux, 1989.

Peck, Elizabeth S., and Emily Ann Smith. *Berea's First 125 Years*. Lexington, KY: University Press of Kentucky, 1982.

Penrose, Roger. *The Emperor's New Mind*. New York: Oxford University Press, 1989.

Peter, Dr. Laurence J. *Peter's Quotations: Ideas for Our Time*. New York: Bantam Books/Bantam Doubleday Dell, 1977.

Pirsig, Robert M. *Zen and the Art of Motorcycle Maintenance: An Inquiry into Values*. New York: Quill/William Morrow, 1979.

Platt, John R. "Strong Inference: Certain Systematic Methods of Scientific Thinking May Produce Much More Rapid Progress Than Others." *Science* (October 1964).

Popcorn, Faith. *The Popcorn Report*. New York: Doubleday, 1991.

Price, David. *Before the Bulldozer: The Nambiquara Indians and the World Bank*. Cabin John, Md.: Seven Locks Press, 1989.

Reid, Thomas. "An Inquiry into the Human Mind on the Principles of Common Sense." Orig. Pub. 1764, in *Inquiry and Other Essays,* ed. by Keith Lehrer and Ronald E. Beanblossom, Indianapolis: Bobbs-Merrill, 1975.

Rich, Bruce. *Mortgaging the Earth: The World Bank, Environmental Impoverishment, and the Crisis of Development*. Boston: Beacon Press, 1993.

———. "The Emperor's New Clothes: The World Bank and Environmental Reform." *World Policy Journal* (Spring 1990).

——— "Conservation Woes at the World Bank." *The Nation* (January 23, 1989).

Riemer, Jeffrey W. "Deviance as Fun." *Adolescence* (Spring 1981).

Robinson, Gail L Nemetz. *Cross Cultural Understanding*. Hertfordshire, U.K.: Prentice-Hall International, 1988.

Roiser, Martin. "Commonsense, Science and Public Opinion." *Journal for the Theory of Social Behavior* (December 1987).

Russell, Bertrand. *Human Knowledge: Its Scope and Limits*. New York: Touchstone/Simon & Schuster, 1948.

Salvia, John, and James E. Ysseldyke. *Assessment in Special and Remedial Education*. Boston: Houghton Mifflin, 1985.

Schank, Roger C. *Tell Me a Story: A New Look at Real and Artificial Memory*. New York: Charles Scribner's Sons, 1991.

Schutz, John A. "Common Sense." *The Encyclopedia Americana: International Edition.* Danbury, Conn.: Grolier, 1992.

Simpson, Lewis David. *The Relationship of Common Sense Philosophy to Hawthorne, Poe, and Melville.* New York: Dissertation Abstracts International (July 1987).

Skinner, B. F. *About Behaviorism.* New York: Knopf, 1974.

Sternberg, Robert J., and Richard K. Wagner. "Tacit Knowledge and Intelligence in the Everyday World." in *Practical Intelligence: Nature and Origin of Competence in the Everyday World.* New York: Cambridge University Press, 1986.

Thomas, R. Murray. *Comparing Theories of Child Development.* Belmont, Calif.: Wadsworth, 1985.

Todd, Michael. "Two-Headed Teen Chops One Head Off!" *Weekly World News* (November 24, 1992).

Tweedie, Gordon. " 'Common Sense': James to Joyce and the Pragmatic L. Bloom." *James Joyce Quarterly* (Spring 1989).

Veblen, Thorstein. *The Theory of the Leisure Class: An Economic Study of Institutions.* Orig. Pub. 1899. New York: Modern Library, 1934.

Wagner, Richard K., and Robert J. Sternberg. "Tacit Knowledge in Managerial Success." *Journal of Business and Psychology* (Summer 1987).

———. "Practical Intelligence in Real-World Pursuits: the Role of Tacit Knowledge." *Journal of Personality and Social Psychology* (August 1985).

Wederspahn, Gary M. "Don't Get Lost in the Translation." *Hemispheres: The Magazine of United Airlines* (February 1993).

Index